Boot Up Projects

Boot Up Projects

The Daily Telegraph
GUIDE TO DOING SOMETHING
USEFUL WITH YOUR COMPUTER

Rick Maybury

TEXERE
LONDON · NEW YORK

Copyright © 2000 Rick Maybury

First published in Great Britain in 2000 by Orion Business

This edition published by

TEXERE Publishing Limited
71–77 Leadenhall Street
London
EC3A 3DE

Tel: +44 (0)20 7204 3644
Fax: +44 (0)20 7208 6701
www.texerepublishing.com

A subsidiary of

TEXERE LLC
55 East 52nd Street
New York, NY 10055

Tel: +1 (212) 317 5106
Fax: +1 (212) 317 5178

The right of Rick Maybury to be identified as the author of
this work has been asserted by him in accordance with the
Copyright, Designs and Patents Act 1988.

A CIP catalogue record for this book is available from
the British Library

ISBN 1-58799-081-4

Printed and bound in Great Britain by
Creative Print and Design (Wales), Ebbw Vale

Contents

CHAPTER 1

Word processing – Getting started

If pressed, you could probably come up with several good reasons why you've bought a personal computer (PC) – games and the Internet figure prominently on many people's list – but the one application that really makes sense of all that expensive and baffling technology is word processing.

The operating systems Windows 95 and Windows 98 have a very useful built-in word processor program called WordPad – though few users realise they have it, let alone use it. Nowadays most new PCs come with a software suite that includes a powerful word processor such as Microsoft Word or Lotus WordPro. Nevertheless, Windows Word-Pad is well worth getting to know. It shares many key features with Word and other more grown-up word processors. If you haven't yet taken the plunge with Word, or have been thoroughly confused by the vast array of its complicated-looking features, WordPad is a very good place to begin. It can be found by clicking on the Start button, then Programs, then Accessories, and you'll find it at the bottom of the list.

WordPad has more facilities than most users will ever need for creating everyday documents, such as letters, reports or faxes. You could easily use it to write that book you've been planning; in fact it has more features than many top-of-the-line word processors from the late 1980s, and it's a darn sight easier to use.

We'll start with the basics, and look at some more advanced operations later on in this chapter. The biggest advantage a word processor has over a typewriter is the facility to manipulate text before it is committed to paper. In other words, if you make a mistake, or change your mind, you can easily alter what you have written.

Formatting, copying and erasing text

Changing a single word or letter using the backspace key is easy enough, but when it comes to editing whole sentences, paragraphs or larger blocks of text the most useful feature is highlighting.

To highlight text, use the mouse to place the cursor in front of the first letter of the word or words you want to work on, click, hold, and move the cursor to the last letter in the block and release the mouse button.

In WordPad and most variants of Microsoft Word you can highlight a single line, a whole paragraph or the entire document, by putting the mouse pointer into the space before the beginning of a line and clicking the left mouse button once, twice or three times. To remove a highlight, left-click into an empty part of the page area.

Once a word or block of text has been highlighted you can do all kinds of interesting things to it, including moving it around, copying it,

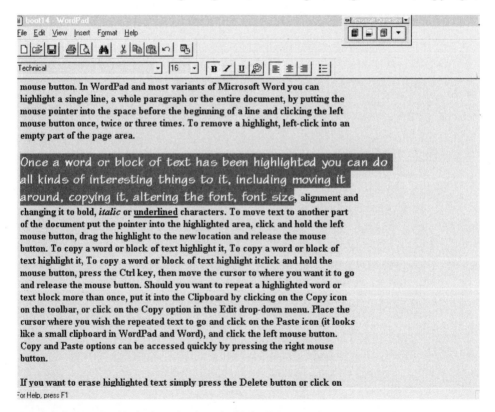

Once a letter, word or block of text has been highlighted you can change the way it looks, move or copy it to another part of the document

altering the font, font size, alignment and changing it to bold, italic or underlined characters.

To move text to another part of the document put the pointer into the highlighted area, click and hold the left mouse button, drag the high-light to the new location and release the mouse button.

To copy a word or block of text highlight it, click and hold the mouse button, press the Ctrl key, then move the cursor to where you want to insert the text and release the mouse button.

To repeat a highlighted word or text block more than once, put it into the Clipboard by clicking on the Copy icon on the toolbar (the two sheets of paper with their corners turned down), or click on the Copy option in the Edit drop-down menu, or press Ctrl + C. Place the cursor where you want the repeated text to go and click on the Paste icon (the small clipboard in WordPad and Word), and click the left mouse button or use the shortcut command Ctrl + V.

Copy and Paste options can be accessed quickly by pressing the right mouse button.

To erase highlighted text, simply press the Delete button or click on the Cut (scissors) icon. If you change your mind about an action, click on the Undo icon (it looks like an arrow curving to the left). MS Word also has a re-do feature (an arrow curving to the right) to change it back again.

Filing

That's really all you need to know to get going, but before you start work on that opus you must organise your filing system, so you don't end up with documents all over the place. Start by creating some empty folders, where you can store your files. It's up to you where you keep them, some word processors will create a work folder for you but it's just as easy to make your own using Windows Explorer.

From Explorer select New, then Folder from the File drop-down menu; you can add a work folder to the list of programs on the C: drive, or create several inside your word processor directory, using names such as letters, personal etc.

You can customise your pages and screen presentation. Options include items like page width, paragraph layout, font, font size and zoom settings, which are normally located on the tool bar or listed under menu items, such as Format. Experiment with the various styles and settings on offer. Once set, the word processor will allow you to save your preferences as the normal or default 'New' document, before you exit the program. In future that's what you will get every time you open a blank page. For security, get into the habit of naming and filing each new document: as soon as you've written the first line click on the File menu and select Save As, give the document a title and make sure it is filed in the correct folder.

Projects

CUSTOMISING WORD

After Windows the next most popular application for PC users has to be Microsoft Word, and it's not difficult to see why. Word is simply the best, and since the very earliest versions this sophisticated word processor program has set the standard by which other word processors are judged. If there has to be a criticism it's that it is too powerful and we suspect most owners never use more than a small fraction of its many features.

We'll begin with a few tips and tweaks to help you get Word up and running, and tailored to suit your needs. Later on we'll delve a bit deeper into some of the more interesting and useful facilities. We're focusing on the two most popular variants of Word: Version 7, which is part of the Office 95 suite of programs, and Word 97, which is included in Office 98 and sold as a stand-alone product. They look very similar but there are several quite significant differences; as far as possible we'll stick to the common features.

Default typeface
Word is reasonably intuitive and even complete novices are usually able to start writing and printing letters or documents after a short time. The first thing most users want to do is customise the blank page that appears when Word starts: this is called the Normal Template. If you don't care for the default typeface or font, and the size of the characters, simply click Format on the menu bar and select Font. Choose

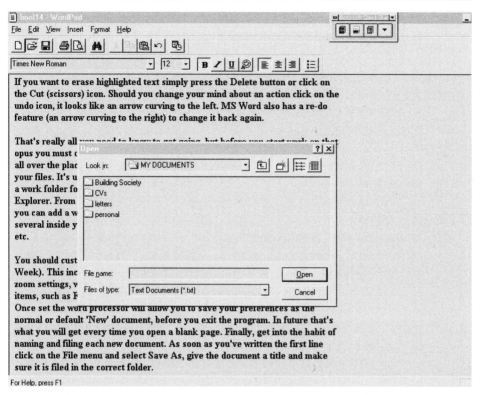

If you want to erase highlighted text simply press the Delete button or click on the Cut (scissors) icon. Should you change your mind about an action click on the undo icon, it looks like an arrow curving to the left. MS Word also has a re-do feature (an arrow curving to the right) to change it back again.

That's really all you need to know to get going, but before you start work on that opus you must c[...] all over the plac[...] your files. It's u[...] a work folder fo[...] Explorer. From [...] you can add a w[...] several inside y[...] etc.

You should cust[...] Week). This inc[...] zoom settings, v[...] items, such as F[...] Once set the word processor will allow you to save your preferences as the normal or default 'New' document, before you exit the program. In future that's what you will get every time you open a blank page. Finally, get into the habit of naming and filing each new document. As soon as you've written the first line click on the File menu and select Save As, give the document a title and make sure it is filed in the correct folder.

Organise your documents by creating a number of subject folders in My Documents

your preferred font, size and style – even the colour if you wish – then click on the Default button, and that's what you'll get every time you open Word.

Toolbars

You can have as many or as few Toolbars on show as you like; however, most of them just waste valuable screen space, with functions you're unlikely to need more than once in a blue moon. The two most useful ones are Standard and Formatting; they're worth keeping on screen all the time. The Toolbar display option is on the View menu, or put the mouse pointer into a toolbar, right click and the selection menu appears. The Toolbars and Menu bar can be shifted around by pointing at the border, clicking and holding the mouse button and then dragging it to where you want it to go.

Screen colours

If paper-white screen in Word becomes tiring on the eyes, you can adjust the screen brightness or, better still, give it a light grey tint. Go to Windows Control Panel (Start, then Settings), click on the Display icon then select the Appearance tab. Click in the Window Text box and go down to the Colour box, which should show white. Click the down arrow on the box and the Other button. Use the vertical slider next to the multi-colour panel to select a light tint and click OK.

Saving documents

First time users often get themselves into a tangle when it comes to saving documents, so get organised as soon as possible. By default all of the files you create will be saved in a directory called My Documents, which exists outside Word, on the main C: drive directory tree. The first job is to work out the various types or categories of documents and letters you'll be creating, 'Personal', 'Bank', 'Letters to Bill Gates', that sort of thing. It's a good idea to put the year after each one (and resolve to create a new set of folders every year). Now go to the Start button, then Programs and Windows Explorer and scroll down the list in the left hand window until you get to My Documents, double click on it and select New from the File Menu and click on the File icon. Create as many folders as you require, re-naming each one as you go. Get into the habit of naming and saving a document in the appropriate folder – using the Save As command in the File menu – as soon as you've written the first line or two.

Spelling and grammar

Word can help you with your spelling by highlighting words it doesn't recognise in red and correcting simple mistakes, as you type. Word also checks grammar and punctuation; this can be a bit hit and miss but it keeps you on your toes and anything it disagrees with is underlined in green. Going to Options in the Tools menu and selecting the Spelling & Grammar tab enables both facilities. This menu decides how the checks work; there's a more in-depth selection of options under Auto-Correct, also on the Tools menu. Spend some time with these menus, ticking the features you consider worthwhile. Don't rely on Auto-Correct, always run a complete spellcheck when you've finished a document by placing the cursor at the beginning of the text and clicking the 'ABC' button on the Toolbar, or clicking on Tools and then Spelling and Grammar.

Counting words

Word Count is something you'll probably want to access often. You can save time by assigning this and any other frequently used functions a simple keyboard shortcut. Select Customize from the Tools menu, click on the Commands tab and then the Keyboard button. In the left-hand window locate and highlight Tools, and in the right window scroll down the list until you come to ToolsWordCount and highlight that. Click a flashing cursor into the 'Press New Shortcut Key' window and choose a simple two-key combination (Ctrl + backslash – next to 'z' on most keyboards – is normally unassigned and simple to do with the left hand); click Assign and it's done.

While you're at it, have a look through the lists of commands and see if there's anything else you want to have a shortcut to. Don't do too many, or you will have trouble remembering them all.

Be creative

Be creative with your letters and faxes; there are plenty of embellishments in Word, so get to know them. You'll find a useful assortment of ready-made templates in Style Gallery under the Format menu; these can be applied when you have finished keying in the text. Try adding borders, you will find a good selection of styles on the Format menu, under Borders & Shading. The same menu bar also has options for drop capitals, plus bullet points and paragraph numbering, though it's easier to use the buttons on the Standard toolbar for the latter two features. Don't forget you can add pictures and graphics to your documents: a good way to learn about this feature is to experiment with the Clip Art facility, which is accessed from the Picture option on the Insert menu.

CREATING LABELS

If you write a lot of letters, or you regularly prepare and send out mailshots, there are some features in Word you really should get to know. On the Tools menu there's an item called Envelopes and Labels. The Envelope tab allows you to print directly onto envelopes, but it can be

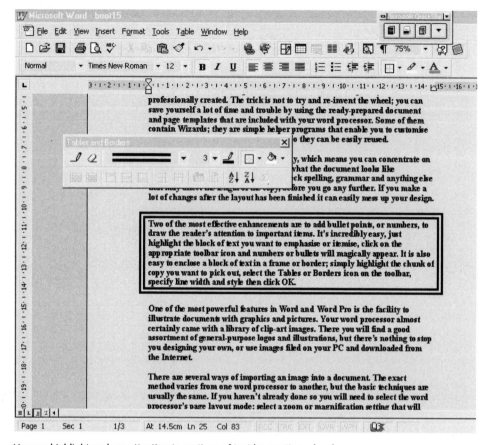

professionally created. The trick is not to try and re-invent the wheel; you can save yourself a lot of time and trouble by using the ready-prepared document and page templates that are included with your word processor. Some of them contain Wizards; they are simple helper programs that enable you to customise [...]o they can be easily reused.

[...]y, which means you can concentrate on [...]vhat the document looks like [...]ck spelling, grammar and anything else [...]fore you go any further. If you make a lot of changes after the layout has been finished it can easily mess up your design.

> Two of the most effective enhancements are to add bullet points, or numbers, to draw the reader's attention to important items. It's incredibly easy, just highlight the block of text you want to emphasise or itemise, click on the appropriate toolbar icon and numbers or bullets will magically appear. It is also easy to enclose a block of text in a frame or border; simply highlight the chunk of copy you want to pick out, select the Tables or Borders icon on the toolbar, specify line width and style then click OK.

One of the most powerful features in Word and Word Pro is the facility to illustrate documents with graphics and pictures. Your word processor almost certainly came with a library of clip-art images. There you will find a good assortment of general-purpose logos and illustrations, but there's nothing to stop you designing your own, or use images filed on your PC and downloaded from the Internet.

There are several ways of importing an image into a document. The exact method varies from one word processor to another, but the basic techniques are usually the same. If you haven't already done so you will need to select the word processor's page layout mode: select a zoom or magnification setting that will

You can highlight or draw attention to sections of text by creating a border

a fairly tedious business especially if you've got a lot of them, and some printers make heavy weather of it. Select the Label tab for the easier and faster alternative.

Sheets of sticky-back labels are readily available from stationers and they're relatively inexpensive, particularly if you buy the own-label brands. There's a huge range of standard 'Avery' styles plus specialist designs, for floppy disks, videocassettes, name badges and even business cards.

From Envelopes and Labels select the Labels tab and click on the Options button. Scroll down the list until you find the type or style of label you're using; if it's not included you can manually key in the dimensions by clicking New Label. At this point you have several options, you can make a sheet of labels with one address repeated, or create a custom sheet containing your own selection of addresses. In that case check the 'Full Page of the Same Label' option (yes, we know it doesn't make sense …) then click on the New Document button. This will bring up a blank sheet of labels, with the outlines marked. Click a cursor into each box and key in the addresses, save and print the sheet as required. It's a good idea to do a test run on an ordinary sheet of paper first, to make sure the text is correctly aligned.

CREATING YOUR OWN STATIONERY

Even quite modest embellishments, such as a letterhead or logo, can make your correspondence really stand out. A few simple design flourishes can add weight or humour to your message, convey a sense of professionalism, catch the reader's eye and greatly improve the chances of it being read and you receiving a response.

Of course, you could pop down to your local print shop and have them run off a few hundred off-the-shelf letterheads, compliments slips and business cards. On the other hand, you could mobilise the quite formidable design and printing facilities within your PC, and do the job yourself. Not only will you have the satisfaction of creating your own unique personal stationery, it will cost a fraction of what a print shop will charge. There's no need to wait for your order to be fulfilled, you print stationery as you need it and there's little or no waste as you can make instant alterations should your home or business address and contact numbers change.

Headed notepaper

We'll begin with headed notepaper. If you're using a reasonably up-to-date word processor such as Microsoft Word or Lotus WordPro, then a lot of the hard work has been done for you. In Word go to the File menu, click on New and select the Letters and Faxes tab. There are some really good designs in there, complete with shading and a well chosen blend of typefaces; all you have to do is substitute your name or company name in the text fields. In WordPro select the New Document item on the File menu and choose one of the preset styles.

Ready-made templates are fine, but it's much more satisfying to create a design from scratch, or borrow elements from the templates by copying and pasting them to a blank page. You can also incorporate facilities like automatic date fields using the AutoText and Field options on the Insert menu in Word. Similar features are available in WordPro on the Text menu, under Insert Other. Both Word and WordPro come with extensive clip art libraries, stuffed full of interesting and useful graphics and logos that can be pasted into your letterhead.

There's nothing to stop you designing your own graphics using the Paint program in Windows or any other paint-box program. You can also import images using a scanner or digital camera (see Chapter 4). Don't be afraid to experiment with typefaces and sizes, though avoid using too many different styles on the same page as it can end up looking messy. When your blank letterhead is complete give it a name and save it as a Document Template (*.dot) file in the Letters and Faxes folder in Word; in WordPro they're saved as SmartMaster files with the extension *.mwp.

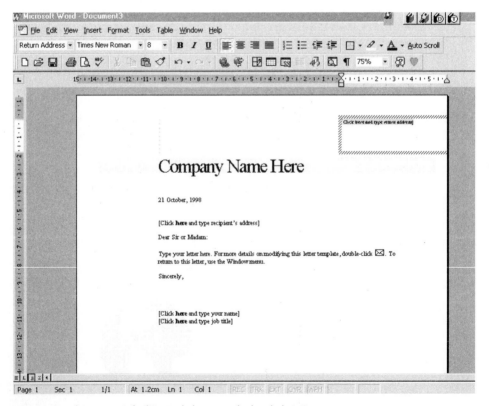

Use your word processer's facilities to help you make headed stationery

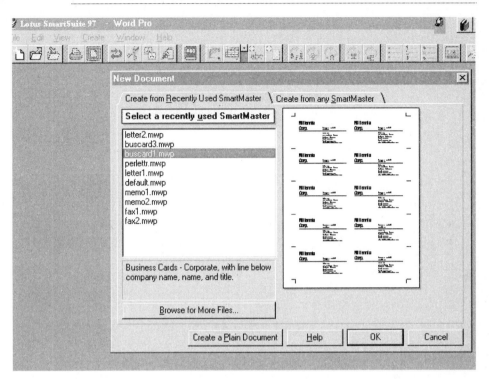

The business card wizard in Lotus WordPro has a number of ready-made templates

Compliments slips

Compliments slips can be based on your letterhead. Omit the date line and any other unnecessary elements and key in any additional text you deem necessary. Rearrange the design so that four slips can be printed on a sheet of A4 paper. When you're happy with it use copy and paste to repeat the design. Save it as a document template, run off a few sheets and cut them into strips, so they're ready for use.

Use the best-quality paper you can lay your hands on for headed stationery and comps slips. Make sure you get the right type (i.e. inkjet or laser) for your printer. Inkjet printing on coarse or highly absorbent paper looks dreadful: the ink runs and characters look ragged.

Business cards

DIY business cards used to be a bit of a problem for PC owners, not because of any deficiency on the part of computers but due to the

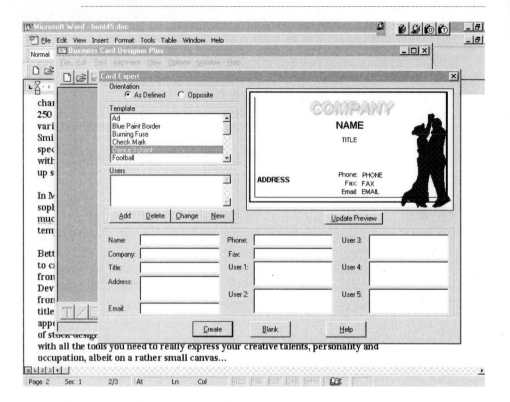

Programs like Business Card Designer Plus can help you to make
professional looking cards

paper handling characteristics of printers. Nowadays most inkjets and
lasers can print on 200 to 250 gsm card, which is well suited to this type
of job. Packs of A4 sized card in various colours are available from stationery shops. You can also buy sheets of micro-perforated blank business cards from specialist suppliers; they're designed to be used with
the label-making software in word processors. It's a lot easier than cut-
ting up sheets of card by hand.

In Word the label facility is on the Tools menu. It's not especially
sophisticated, though it is possible to produce a plain and simple card
without too much trouble. WordPro goes one better with a small selection of business card templates, which can be found in Smart Masters
in the New Document menu.

Better still, there are a number of programs on the market specifically
designed to create fancy-looking business cards. Two of the best known

are CardBase, from Software By Design, and Business Card Designer Plus from CAM Development. Fully functioning 30-day trial/shareware versions are available from a number of sites on the Internet (Business Card Designer Plus http://hotfiles.zdnet.com and CardBase http://www.execpc.com). Both titles are very easy to use. You start by entering the information you want to appear on the card, after that you can see what it will look like using the supply of stock designs. However, they're really mini desk-top publishing programs with all the tools you need to express your creative talents, personality and occupation, albeit on a rather small canvas.

Q&A Real world problems

Customs check

Q   My son has been using Word on our home PC to do his school homework. I noticed him select the assistance of the spellchecker. To my dismay he hit the 'Add' button to save incorrectly spelled words. He now tells me that this is his usual practice. How can I get into the dictionary to correct these additions?
A. G. via e-mail

A   User defined spellings in Word are contained in an editable text file called 'Custom.dic'. You can access it from within Word by going to File, Open and in the 'Look in' field select Hard Disk C:, then go to Program Files > Common Files > Microsoft Shared > Proof > Custom.dic, or it might be in Program Files > Microsoft Office > Office. Once it's on the screen you can add, delete or change entries before saving the file.

Cast a spell

Q   I want to change incorrect spellings in the main dictionary (yes, there are some!). Where do I find it and how do I correct it?
A. M. via e-mail

A   You can't, at least not directly, because the file is 'hard coded' and there's no way to get at it, but you can impose your will upon the dictionary by making it spell words the way you want them to be. Click on Help then Contents and Index, select the Index tab, type in Dictionaries, double click on dictionaries (spelling), then select 'Specify a preferred spelling for a word'. This will bring up instructions on how to create an exclusion dictionary.

Drawing the line

Q   I have a problem, which must drive millions round the bend. Have you tried drawing a single or double line across a decimal tab so that, like any neat accountant wishes, one can single overline, and double underline the figure before the decimal point, the decimal point and the figures after the decimal point?

In Windows 3.1 there used to be a useful typeface MSLinedraw which, by using insert symbol, one could find a single line and double line which would look neat and tidy. In Windows 95/98/NT that has apparently been 'designed out' (according to the Microsoft Knowledge Network) and, by a great deal of searching, one can find those symbols in the 'Courier New' typeface. However, whichever typeface one uses the line can still not be made to go across a decimal tab so that a continuous line is obtained over the whole number, the decimal point and the decimal figures. Any suggestions?

N. H. via e-mail

A   There are several options. Put the figures in a borderless table and then put a single-line bottom border to the cell under the last number to be totalled and a double line bottom border in the cell with the total or final figure. You can also use Drawing Tools. Click on the 'Draw' icon, choose the line tool, hold down shift to ensure a smooth, straight line, and draw the line where you want it. You can also highlight the figure and press Ctrl + shift + D. The overline can be added by selecting and underlining the figure in the line above (or adding a line and typing underlined spaces. Incidentally, spaces to the right of the decimal tab won't underline so instead of using the spacebar alone, key Ctrl + shift + spacebar) non-breaking space.

By the numbers

Q I read somewhere that it was possible to change the format of page numbering in Microsoft Word in order that it would show, for example, 'Page 3 of 10' rather than the single number option currently offered. I am unable to locate the document and cannot for the life of me remember how to do it.
A. M. via e-mail

A Go to View on the menu bar and select Header and Footer. Decide whether you want the page number to appear at the top or bottom of the page by clicking the cursor into the dotted Header or Footer box on the page. Next, click the Insert AutoText button on the Header and Footer toolbar, scroll down the list and select the Page X of Y option.

Date dilemma

Q I frequently use preformatted letters in both MS Word and Works files, where I make use of the facility to insert today's date. The problem is after saving these letters when I want to review them, they appear with the current date on reopening and I can't find the date on which they were originally written. How can I store the original date without having to manually type it on all letters?
M. S. via e-mail

A The auto date facility in a Word document template is generated by a hidden 'field code' and unless it is locked or unlinked, it will always show the current date. It's easy to disable, click on the date and it should be highlighted in grey, now press Ctrl + Shift + F9 and it will turn black – i.e. a normal highlight – confirming that it has been turned into plain text, which will not now change.

Accursed date

Q Every time I type the date for a letter in Word 97 (in the form: date, month, year) a rectangle briefly appears reading, for instance '1999-04-01' (it's even done it just now ...). Not only does this very irritating item appear but it prints it out of its own accord. How do I rid myself of this accursed thing?

E. H. London W4

A   It's called an 'AutoComplete Tip', it's another one of those supposedly helpful little features – usually installed by default – that drive some PC users crazy because the means to switch them off is often difficult to find. In this case the option to disable it lives on the Insert menu under AutoText, select AutoText on the sub menu that appears, select the AutoText tab and uncheck the box marked 'Show AutoComplete Tip …'

Vulgar Type

Q   I have Windows 98 with MS Word. How do I write vulgar fractions, such as 3/16, etc. or any other figure, but written with a horizontal dividing line, with the enumerator above and the dividend below? According to Help I should key in Ctrl\F, but that gets Find.

T. R. Hants

A   Help isn't very helpful in this case: what it is describing is an equation field code, but it doesn't go into enough detail. There is an easy way, however, and that is to go to the Insert drop-down menu and select Field, in the Categories Window click on Equations and Formulas and in the Field Names window highlight EQ. In the Field Code window the letters EQ appear. Insert a cursor after the letters and type: '\f(a,b)' (leaving out the inverted commas) where the letters 'a' and 'b' represent the enumerator and dividend respectively, and don't forget the comma. Click OK and the fraction will be inserted into the document. You can reduce the size using the typeface commands on the Formatting toolbar.

Wherefore art thou Euro?

Q   I am informed that somewhere in the oceanic depths of Windows 98 there resides the Euro symbol. Could you please verify that it is available in Windows?

Also can it be used as a normal font (i.e. change size, boldness etc.) Or, if it is available as a download from the Internet, where can it be found?

D. S. via e-mail

A   The Euro symbol is included in the 'core' fonts used by Windows 98. The default keyboard shortcuts are Alt Gr + 4 (the right hand Alt key) and Ctrl + Alt + 4. If you are using a word processor like MS Word, you can also find it in the Symbol table on the Insert menu. It is on the Currency subset under 'Normal Text'. Since the critical core fonts are 'TrueType' you can treat the Euro symbol like any other character and change all or any of its attributes. Users of older versions of Windows can download updated font sets from the Microsoft web site at: http://www.microsoft.com/typography/fontpack/default.htm.

Dotty about Zoë

Q   I have a small problem. My daughter's name is Zoë with two dots over the ë. My problem is this; every time I want to type her name in a Word document I type Z-O-E. Word then underlines this spelling as incorrect and offers me a number of options, the second of which is the correct spelling. As I type her name frequently this can be very frustrating and time-consuming. How can I insert the diaeresis without spellchecking? Would it affect just Zoe or all words with an e and two dots, such as Noel? If it is easy for a single letter then perhaps I could do it for words with an 'i' which also have a diaeresis, such as naïve and Aïda?

D. F. London NW2

A   You can use Word's AutoCorrect facility to make sure the modified character appears as you write. Type in Zoe then run the spellchecker. Highlight the spelling you want to use then click on the AutoCorrect button. To automatically insert special characters into other words go to the Insert menu and click on Symbol. Highlight the character you wish to use then click the AutoCorrect button. Enter the word, as you would normally type it in the Replace field, click the 'With' checkbox, and type in the word you want to appear, using the special character. Select Add and it's done. Alternatively type 'Z' then 'o' then Alt + 0235 (on the number pad) that gives the ë. You can also get a vowel with an umlaut in Microsoft Word by holding Ctrl, shift and ':' (colon), release, then hit the vowel key as either upper or lower case.

Easy accents

Q   Is there a way of inserting grave, circumflex and acute accents as well as cedillas in Microsoft Word?
P. W. via e-mail

A   If you are using a word processor like MS Word or Lotus WordPro you will find details of all available accented characters in Help, under Special Characters. In Word, for example, you just select Symbol from the Insert menu and either double click on the character to insert it into a document, or assign it a keyboard shortcut if it is going to be used frequently. You can also use an ANSI (American National Standards Institute) code to generate accented characters, by pressing and holding the ALT key and using the keypad (with Num lock enabled) to enter the relevant code. You can find this by going to Start > Programs > Accessories > System Tools > Character Map. There you will find a full set of characters for each font. Highlight the character or symbol and its ANSI code or keyboard assignment will appear in the bottom right-hand corner of the window.

Another method is to use shortcut keys on the International Character table. Go to Help on the Start menu and type 'characters', double-click 'special' and select Type International Characters.

Pole positions

Q   I have been an MS Word user for many years, but have reverted to DOS-based WordPerfect for the character sets that I require when I write to my Polish relatives. The Polish language requires extra letters with a dot above z, acute accents on the c, n, o, s and z, the crossed l, and a right-hand hook below the a and e. These are all available with WordPerfect, but I cannot find them using MS Word 6.0 and Windows 95. Are they there but hidden?
A. W. via e-mail

A   On the Insert menu in Word 6 select Symbol, type in the name of the font that you are using in WordPerfect (that contains the special characters) and press Return. You can then insert the characters into a document by double-clicking, or assign them keyboard shortcuts. You could also try using the Character Map utility (Start > Programs > Accessories), which will also give you the character's ANSI code, so you can enter it in any application by pressing the Alt key plus the indicated 4-digit code.

Fast fonts

Q   There are times when it is difficult to choose which font to use in Word 7. The drop-down menu in Microsoft Publisher shows an example of the font. Is it possible to see an example of Microsoft Word fonts on screen or to print a test page for easy reference?
    G. W. via e-mail

A   Word 6 and Word for Windows (aka Word 7) come with a macro called FontSampleGenerator that will print out examples of all of the fonts on your PC (and supported by the printer), see Help for details, and if necessary run the set-up program again. A similar macro is also available for Word 97, though it is not supplied as standard and you will have to download it from the Microsoft web site (http://support.microsoft. com/support/kb/articles/Q170/9/70.asp). It's quite long so highlight, copy and paste the macro text from the web page into an empty macro field (Tools > Macros > Create call it ListFonts).

It's all Greek...

Q   I have two questions relating to Windows 98 and MS Word. The Find and Replace facility would be more useful if it could be used to correct and replace symbols, Greek letters or other characters included in the Symbols tariff. Can this be done?
    How can I obtain the soft and hard breathings and other diacritics used in classical Greek, but not included in the Modern Greek alphabet under Symbols?
    D. B. Surrey

A   Find and Replace works with any character or symbol. Simply copy and paste the symbol (highlight and press Ctrl + C to copy, Ctrl + V to paste) from your document into the Find field, and type or copy and paste the symbol or character you want to substitute into the Replace With box.

There are several web sites on the Internet dealing with the tricky subject of classical and Modern Greek accents, with downloadable fonts, templates macros. Try: http://www.classics.ox.ac.uk/software/old-greek macropage.html; http://www.isr.umd.edu/~kanlis/Greek/Font/stressin. htm; http://www.doctor-flynn.demon.co.uk/accents.htm

Slow word

Q   My Word 97 program has developed this infuriating fault. If I save and close the current page, instead of disappearing immediately it takes about 12 seconds before it closes. I've tried uninstalling and re-installing with no success.
J. W. via e-mail

A   If you are using Office 97 it could be that Outlook is automatically creating a journal entry – this can still happen even if Outlook is not running. In Outlook on the Tools menu select Options and the Journal tab, clear all of the check boxes in the 'Also record files from' list and click OK.

Office irritant

Q   Recently, I was delighted to discover how to stop automatic date insertion in Word. Now can you tell me how to get rid of that darned Office Assistant who always assumes I need his help to write a letter?
J. P. via e-mail

A   Click on the Office Assistant icon on the toolbar and then the Options button; on the Options tab uncheck Display Alerts. However, the only way to get rid of it permanently is to uninstall it from Word. You'll need your Office or Word CD-ROM, go to Control Panel and

Add/Remove programs, click on Office 97 or Word 97 and then on Add/Remove. This starts the Word uninstall programme. Click on Remove Components, then Office Accessories; this leads to a window that displays all of the add-on components. Deselect Office Assistant from the list that appears and click on Continue to remove it. A slightly less drastic solution is to open Windows Explorer/Program Files/Microsoft Office/Office, then right click on the folder named Actors and rename it Dead_Actors.

Super solution

Q   Can you tell me how to get subscript characters in Word? This is required when writing chemical formula/symbols such as H_2O or CO_2. Is there a reference list of all these various codes?
P. C. via e-mail

A   Hold down Ctrl and Shift keys then press the '=' key to toggle super-script on or off. Ctrl + Caps Lock + '=' does the same for subscript. Alternatively you can set up buttons on the tool bar. Right click on the tool bar area and, on the menu that opens click 'Customise'. In the 'Commands' section highlight 'Format' and find, in turn, 'Superscript' and 'Subscript' in the list on the right of the window. Left click on each and drag the icon onto the tool bar.

CHAPTER 2 **Design and layout**

*Word processors aren't just for text; some of them
are pretty good with pictures and graphics as well...*

Word processor programs such as Microsoft Word have a number of powerful presentation tools, which can give your CVs, letters, faxes, reports and newsletters extra visual impact, to make them look as though they were professionally created. The trick is not to try and re-invent the wheel: you can save yourself a lot of time and trouble by using the ready-prepared document and page templates that are included with your word processor. Some of them contain wizards – simple helper programs that enable you to customise the template to your own specifications, so they can easily be reused.

All of the tools can be used retrospectively, which means you can concentrate on keying in the text first, and worry about what the document looks like afterwards. That's important: always check spelling, grammar and anything else that may affect the length of the copy before you go any further. If you make a lot of changes after the layout has been finished it can easily mess up your design.

Two of the most effective enhancements are to add bullet points or numbers to draw the reader's attention to important items. It's incredibly easy: just highlight the block of text you want to emphasise or itemise, click on the appropriate toolbar icon and numbers or bullets will magically appear.

It is also easy to enclose a block of text in a frame or border: simply highlight the chunk of copy you want to pick out, select the Tables or Borders icon on the toolbar, specify line width and style then click OK.

One of the most powerful features in Word and WordPro is the facility to illustrate documents with graphics and pictures. Your word processor almost certainly came with a library of clip art images. There you will find a good assortment of general-purpose logos and illustrations, but there's nothing to stop you designing your own, or use images filed on your PC and downloaded from the Internet.

There are several ways of importing an image into a document. The exact method varies from one word processor to another, but the basic techniques are usually the same. If you haven't already done so you will need to select the word processor's page layout mode; select a zoom or magnification setting that will allow you to see at least half to two-thirds of the page (if you choose a full-page display, and you're using a small monitor [14 or 15 inches] you won't be able to read the copy or see the images clearly). This will also show you exactly what the finished page will look like when it is printed out.

Using the cursor or mouse pointer decide where you want the illustration to go on the page. In Word 7 images are chosen using the Picture option on the Insert menu. From there you can search through the Clip Art library. Incidentally, additional clip art can be downloaded free from the Microsoft web site by clicking on the browser button in the bottom right hand of the dialogue box. There's tons more of it to be found spread around the Internet. Otherwise you can search for a specific image file, located elsewhere on your computer, using the familiar directory tree.

When you've decided on an image, double-click on it and it will be imported into the open word processor document. Initially the picture will be highlighted, so that it can be moved around the page using the mouse pointer, and if necessary re-sized, by clicking, holding and dragging on one of the squares on the corners of the picture.

Alternatively, load the image into the Windows 95 Paint program (filed in the Accessories folder) or any other paint-box or image manipulation software program that you may have. From the Edit menu, copy the image to the clipboard, then return to the word processor and paste it into the document, from where you can position and resize it.

Word processors such as Microsoft Word have a powerful text wrapping facility that can run the words around the picture. On Word 7 it is located on the Format menu under the heading Object, though it only appears when an image has been highlighted. Click on the Wrapping tab, and from the selections presented, choose how you want the text to surround the picture. It's actually a lot easier than it sounds; nevertheless, it pays to do a few dry runs, before trying anything too ambitious.

Projects

CREATING A NEWSLETTER

Producing a newsletter is easy, the trouble is most word processing and desk-top publishing (DTP) programs have far too many options and inevitably some early efforts end up looking like a dog's dinner. So, the first thing to do is open a new page on your word processor, select a big bold typeface and type 'KEEP IT SIMPLE !', print it out and stick it somewhere you can see it.

Word processing programs such as Microsoft Word have everything you need to create a really professional looking newsletter. However, if you're going to be doing a lot of them or want to prepare a succession of longer multi-page documents it is worth investing in some inexpensive DTP software, such as Adobe Pagemaker, MS Publisher or Serif Page Plus.

We'll begin with the simplest method, which is to use your word processor to transform ready prepared text, a club or society report for example, into an illustrated newsletter. For this example we'll be using MS Word, though the basic principles can be applied to most recent word processing programs. Start by opening the text file and select the Page Layout option from the View menu; a 75% zoom setting should allow you to see between half and two-thirds of the page on a 14 or 15-inch monitor. You will probably find that 9 or 10 point justified text produces the best-looking results. Next, highlight all the text by putting the mouse pointer into the space to the left of the copy and click the left mouse button three times. Go to the Column icon on the toolbar (or Columns on the Format menu, for a wider choice of styles) and choose a two or three column layout from the options presented. Three column designs look cleaner and allow more flexibility with pictures and illustrations. You will see that the copy flows from one column to the next. If you make changes to column one, say, then any over or underflow words will be pushed into or drawn back from the next columns, and onto any subsequent pages.

Now create a banner or title by going to the Insert menu and clicking on Text Box. The mouse pointer will change to a pair of crosshairs; position it on the first letter in column one, click and hold the left

Keep it simple – try to limit the number of typefaces and font sizes and break up text using lines and borders

mouse button and create a rectangular box by dragging the crosshair across the top of the page. The body text will move down the page to make way for the box and a flashing cursor will appear inside the box when you release the mouse button. Type in your banner or title, press return and key in any other information you want to appear at the head of the page, such as a sub-title, the date, volume and issue numbers. Highlight each item and select the appropriate typeface and font size. You will probably have to experiment with the typeface setting and the size of the box, to get everything in.

If you haven't already done so, insert some headlines into the copy, to separate the various items. You can do this by highlighting and enlarging body text, or inserting text boxes. Do not be tempted to use a different typeface for headlines – remember Keep it simple – otherwise it can look messy. To make headlines stand out use bold characters and/or capital letters.

Adding pictures to your page is very straightforward. From the Insert menu click on Picture and select From File or Clip Art; the From File option will take you to the directory tree, so you can retrieve an image from another application, such as an art program, scanner or digital camera picture library. When you have located the image file double-click on it, and it will be placed on the page and displace the text. Use the mouse to move it to the correct position, and the sizing boxes around the image, to fit it into the space. You can use the Crop facility on the Picture sub-menu to trim the image.

If you want to caption the picture, insert a Text Box beneath it; it's usually a good idea to use a slightly smaller typeface (a point or two less than the body text, and make it bold, so that it stands out). You needn't worry too much about alignment. Text boxes, pictures and any other objects you place on the page will automatically 'snap' to line up with an invisible grid.

Sod's law says that there's always too much, or not enough text to neatly fill a page. The former can be solved with some judicious editing, or if you can't bear to cut your masterwork, try reducing the font size by a point, though don't go below 9 points for body copy if you can help it. Filling an empty space is just as easy. Either write some more copy, increase the point size, or better still, create a 'Callout', by inserting a quote or sentence from the text across one or two columns. That's also a good way of drawing the reader's attention to a particular point.

Time to add a few finishing touches. Inserting lines between the columns helps break up the page and make it look more interesting. This facility is on the Drawing menu. Position the mouse pointer where you want the line to begin, click and hold the left mouse button and drag the line to where you want it to end. Check the line is straight and release the button. Don't worry if it's too long or short, you can change it by clicking on the sizing box at the end of the line. Create a small text box at the foot of the page and type in a page number, you may want

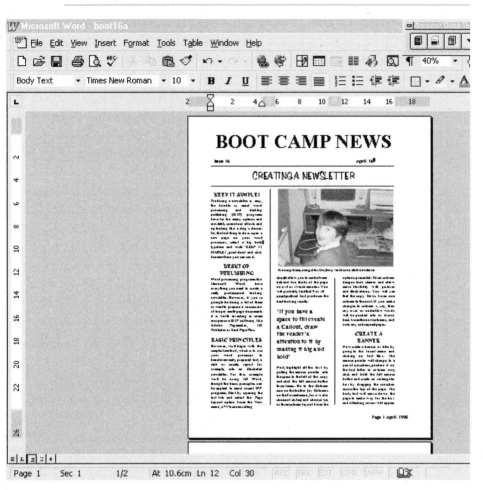

Use the Page View mode or click the Print Preview icon to see how it will look when it's printed

to add the month and year or any other information you feel is relevant.

Use the whole page mode or press the Print Preview icon to see on screen what your page will look like. When your happy with your efforts, run off a page proof on the printer, read it through, get someone else to double check it for you, correct any mistakes and roll the presses.

DESIGNING YOUR OWN CHRISTMAS CARDS

If you've got a PC and a colour inkjet printer your Christmas card problems are solved – make your own! Designing and printing your own cards probably won't save you a huge amount of money, though it will be cheaper than going to a print bureau, and DIY cards have a number of advantages over the store-bought variety: it's personal, people appreciate and remember the thought, and if you're running a business a corporate Christmas card is an excellent opportunity to send greetings to clients and customers, with a touch of humour (possibly with a discrete commercial message as well, but we won't get into that …). You only need to print as many as you need, so there's less waste, and if you're not making too many you could personalise each one with the recipient's name or a short note.

Everything you need to create a basic greetings card is included in Windows 95 and 98, though if you want to do a really bang-up job, and make your life easier, one or two extra items of software and hardware might come in useful. Up-to-date word processors, such as Microsoft Word or Lotus WordPro, have good page layout facilities and a graphics program, such as PaintShop Pro (available as try before you buy shareware from www.jasc.com and computer magazine cover-mount CD-ROMs) will assist with the artwork. If you have a digital camera, scanner or an Internet connection then you will have much greater choice of imagery to work with. Incidentally, scanners often come with graphics software that includes greeting card templates; you may well find something there that takes your fancy.

Commercial card designer programs are all very well – and there's plenty to choose from – but it's far more satisfying to make use of what you have so we'll look at two very simple techniques, using standard Windows 95/98 PC software. Which method you choose will depend to a large extent on the capabilities of your printer. Check the manual to find out the maximum weight or thickness of paper it can handle. If you're limited to thinnish paper, 80 – 120 Gsm, say, then a double fold A4 sheet (ending up as an A6 size card) is most suitable. If you can print on 200 to 250 gsm card, then you can produce a gatefold card, making two A6 sized cards per A4 sheet.

If you have to work with A4 paper then the trick is to place the text message and artwork that will appear inside the card, in the lower right-hand quarter of the page. The 'front cover' image or artwork goes in the top right corner. This has to be printed upside down, so that when the page is folded into half, then half again, it will appear on the outside cover the right way up, and the text will be facing you when it is opened. It sounds more complicated than it is; try it with a sheet of A4 paper, fold it twice, mark the front and inside, open it up again and you'll see how it works.

Begin with the front cover artwork. This can come from a variety of sources; you can create a simple design from scratch using the Paint program in Windows (Start, Accessories). Better still, use a scanned

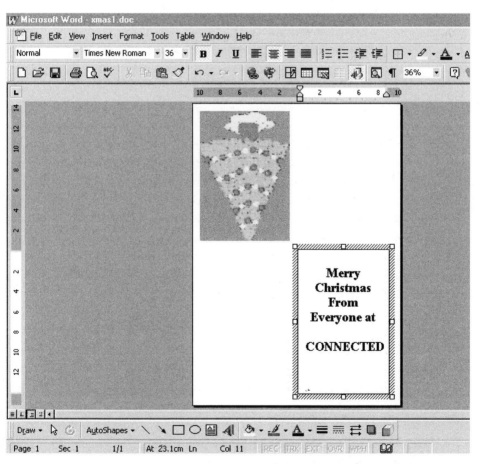

When printing on an A4 sheet of paper, the outside front cover image needs to be upside down, so that it's the right way around when the paper is folded

picture of the family or kids or import some festive clip art from one of the many sites around the Internet. A small selection of useful addresses is:

● http://stega.smoky.org/~habib/cmas.html
● http://members.aol.com/Magic4071/holiday.html
● http://home8.swipnet.se/~w-84551/xmaspage1A.html
● http://www.quantum.si/sejem/jaslice/whatsall.htm

To use an Internet image simply right click on it, choose the Save Picture As option and save it in your document folder. If you are using Paint, save it as a bitmap (*.bmp) file in the Save As Type file window. Open the image in Paint (or your preferred paint-box program), and insert any text as required. When you're happy with it flip or rotate the image (you may have to flip horizontally as well as vertically to make sure text comes out the right way) and save it. Repeat with any other graphics you want on the cover. Now you can paste the artwork into an open document, either by copying it to the clipboard, or using the word processor's Insert Picture option. Position and size the pictures in the top right-hand corner of the page. Insert a text box into the bottom right corner of the page and compose your message. Make a test print, to check alignment and fold lines and amend as necessary.

Printing directly to card requires a slightly different technique. You'll be making two cards at once; moreover the front covers and inside messages are on opposite sides of the paper, so the card has to pass through the printer twice. Once again start with the art-work that's going to appear on the outside. Import it into your open word processor document, this time position it in the top right-hand corner of the page then copy (click to highlight and press Ctrl) and drag or paste a duplicate image immediately underneath – this is easiest in whole page view mode. Next open a second blank page; use the window sizing bars to place it along-side the first, so you can see both pages at once, to check align-ment. Create and position a text box in the top right quarter of the page. Write your message, add any artwork then place a copy underneath.

Print the front cover page first (or pages if you're making a lot of cards) then print the inside message by turning the card over, and

Internet web sites like this one contain lots of festive clip art. To save
a graphic to disk right-click on the image and select the Save Picture
As option

loading it into the printer upside down. It's a good idea to do a test
sheet on ordinary paper first, to make sure everything lines up and
comes out the right way around. When they're finished cut, fold and
sign.

Q&A **Real world problems**

Equation irritation

Q   I am writing a technical article using the Word 97 equation facility. I had produced some seventeen equations and a table, when without warning I was horrified to find that Word had replaced all my equations with black rectangular boxes containing a red line. If I try to edit one of the boxes my equation appears, but if I do anything else, or exit, the box and my equation is replaced by a long line of tiny dots.

   A search through several Word manuals has revealed nothing. This is not the action of a virus, my PC is new, with a virus checker. I only use Microsoft registered software and I have never connected to the Internet. What is going on, and is there a way of recovering my equations?
R. B. Kent

A   There is a known problem with Word 97 displaying generic graphic pictures in place of inserted objects. The cure is to install Microsoft Service Release 1 (SR-1). This can be obtained from the Microsoft web site – details below – and it includes a patch that will stop it happening in future. It may be possible to recover an equation by double clicking on it (to activate it) then try pasting it into a new document, but this procedure is not guaranteed, and only try it after SR-1 has been installed.

   Service Release 1 is available from: http://officeupdate.microsoft.com/downloadDetails/sr1of97zdetail.htm

Transfer list

Q   Help! I want to use my PC to design and print some waterslide transfers using an Epsom 600. This would of course require the appropriate material to print on. Such is either extremely elusive, or simply does not exist.
D. C. via e-mail

A   A quick search on the Internet revealed a number of sources. It's used in the pottery industry for prototyping designs. Have a word with

Tullis Russell Brittains of Stoke-on-Trent; they manufacture A3 and A4 sizes, which sell in packs of 50 for approximately £1.20 a sheet. They can be reached on (01782) 202567, or visit their web site at http://www.brittains.co.uk

Directory enquiry

Q   I have a number of floppy disks, each of which contains a large number of files. I can open the Explorer window showing all of the files on each disk. Is there any way in which this list can be printed to form an index? At the moment I am writing out the list by hand and then retyping it.
R. T. via e-mail

A   There is no direct method of printing from Windows Explorer but here are three ways of achieving the desired result, i.e. creating a printed copy of the contents of a directory or folder on a floppy or the hard disk.

1   Open Windows Explorer, press Alt + Prt Scn and an image of the window – as it appears on the screen – is copied to the Clipboard. Open the Paint program, press Ctrl + V to paste the image and it can be printed using the Print command.

2   Click Start, then Programs and click the MS-DOS icon. In the DOS window that appears type A: (or C: if that's where the directory or files are located). If necessary use the change directory 'cd' command to navigate to the relevant file folder, i.e. type cd\Letters at the C: prompt, where Letters is the name of the folder. If the folder is inside another folder use the cd command again (this time without a backslash) until the full path is displayed, i.e. A:\Letters\Personal. Now enter the following: 'dir > filename.txt' and press return (where filename is the name of the folder or directory you're interested in) and a text file containing a list of the contents of that folder will be created and stored in that folder. You can now close the MS-DOS window and open and print the text document using your word processor.

3   Create a batchfile to print the contents of a directory by opening Notepad and type in: DIR %1 > LPT1 (where LPT1 is your printer port). Use Save As to give it a name, use the extension .bat (i.e. foldprnt.bat), and save it in the root of the C: drive. Now go to the Run command on the Start menu and type C:\foldprnt.bat A:\directory (where A: is the drive where the folder or files are stored [use C: if it's on the hard disk] and directory is the name of the folder whose contents you want to print out). If you just want to print out the list of files on the disk type C:\dirprnt.bat A:

Word picture

Q Please help a comparative newcomer to PCs. I have used Microsoft Word to set up and print a personal letterhead and have also printed photographs via my Plustek Optic Pro scanner. However, I can find no instructions on how to transfer a photo, reduced, onto the letterhead. Can you please guide me?
P. P. via e-mail

A It's easy: first decide where you want the picture to go by clicking a flashing cursor into the open document. Next, from the Insert menu in Word select Picture and click on the From File option and use the directory tree that appears to locate the image. When you have found it click on the listing once and a preview of the picture will appear in the right-hand window. If it's the one you want click OK, Word will change to the Page Layout view and the picture will be imported into your open Word document. Click onto the image to insert sizing squares, so you can move it around and alter its shape and dimensions.

CHAPTER 3 **Tools, tables and numbers**

Deep inside your word processor there are some powerful hidden facilities that are well worth getting to know.

Early word processors were basically electronic typewriters, with the extremely useful facility of being able to manipulate and correct text before it was committed to paper. Over the years many extra bells and whistles have been added, making writing easier and faster, more enjoyable even. However, if you take a close look at any of today's most popular word processors you will find that the original function – putting words on paper – is only one of a plethora of features. The sad thing is lots of people either don't understand what many of them do, or convince themselves that they will never need them.

The trouble is the creators of these highly sophisticated programs seem to be stuck in a kind of timewarp, back when word processors were mostly used by large companies, with the time and resources to train their staff to use them. Today most word processor packages are bought by individuals and small companies. Users are thrown in at the deep end, the manuals supplied with a lot of word processing programs – if you get one at all – are often so rudimentary that it's difficult to progress beyond the basics, or they are so fiendishly complicated they are clearly written by and for experts.

Home PC users and those working for small companies don't have time to go on training courses or wade through half a dozen technical manuals, they want to be able to use their word processors straight away, and to be fair that is exactly what they get. The graphical user interface of Windows has made word processors, indeed most programs, very easy to use, but the downside is that few users stray beyond the core word processing functions and either miss or ignore all of the other goodies they've bought and paid for. In this chapter we're going to delve behind the scenes and look at some of the hidden facilities in your word processor, that you may not even know you had.

Projects

CREATING A VAT INVOICE

Table is one of Word's most powerful functions. In addition to creating very neat looking tables (have a fiddle around with the Table icon on the Toolbar) it can do all sorts of other clever things and it's well worth reading up on the subject. To give you a taste of what is possible we'll create a simple invoice form that automatically calculates totals and VAT.

Open a blank page, click on Insert Table on the table menu, and select 2 columns and 6 rows and click OK. You can choose Autoformat and view the default styles, though for this example a plain grid is best. You can move the vertical lines around by clicking and dragging: to make it look a bit more professional click on the centre line and shift it to the right to make one wide and one narrow column. Table uses the spreadsheet convention of assigning letters and numbers to columns and rows, so our simple table has columns A and B, and rows 1 to 6. Put a cursor in square or 'cell' A4 and type in the words 'Sub total'. In cell A5 type 'VAT at 17.5%', and in cell A6 type 'Total'.

Now click a cursor in square B4, go to the Table drop-down menu and select Formula. In the field marked Formula you should see an equals sign, after it type 'SUM (ABOVE)', omitting the quotation marks; in the Number format box below select the £#... option. This tells the table to add together all the numbers in the column above the cell and display the total after a £ sign. Click on OK. Now click a cursor into cell B5 and go to Formula on the Table menu again. This time after the equals sign type 'B4*17.5%', highlight the £ #... option in the Number format box and click on OK. This instructs the table to take the number that appears in cell B4 and multiply it by 17.5%. Finally, click the cursor into cell B6 and in the appropriate window type after the

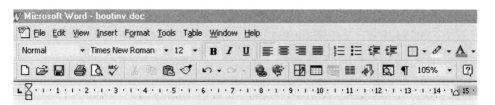

BOOT CAMP ENTERPRISES

INVOICE

77 Acacia Avenue, Thetford, Duncaster, SS78 3DF
Telephone (01234) 778899

Stationery -- 200 A4 labels	£34.22
25 floppy discs	£7.18
Telephone calls	£3.77
Sub Total	£45.17
VAT at 17.5%	£7.90
Total	£53.07

Payment in 30 days is much appreciated

You can create a simple invoice using the table functions in Word

equals sign 'SUM (B4, B5)', to tell the table to add together the contents of cells B4 and B5, and show the total with the £#... number format.

Now you can try it out. Click a cursor into cell B1 and type in a number (pounds and pence) do the same in cells B2 and B3. Put the cursor within the text in cell B5 and you should see a grey box; press the F9 key and the sum of the numbers on column B will appear. Do the same in cell B5 and the computer will work out the VAT. Repeat for cell B6 and the total will be displayed. Add extra information and embellishments to your form as required.

MASTERING MACROS

A macro is a simple program that strings together a set of commands, controlled by a toolbar button, menu selection or keyboard shortcut. There are two ways to create a macro: manually record a set of actions, or write the instructions in a text-based language called WordBasic. The latter is necessary when an action or command isn't available from the keyboard or mouse.

Recording a macro

Recording a macro is the best technique for beginners. The following example creates a button or icon on the toolbar icon, which when you click on it will automatically insert the words 'Best Wishes' in a letter or document.

From the Tools menu select Macro and then click on the Record New Macro item. This opens a dialogue box. Click on the Toolbar icon and another window opens. Click and hold on the triangular icon and drag it to the toolbar; right click on the button and select Change Button Image; choose a design and click OK. Right click on it again and this time choose Default Style; then click on the close button in the Customize window. The dialogue box labelled 'Stop Recording' signifies that every action you make is being recorded. Now go to the Insert menu, select AutoText, then Closing and click on 'Best Wishes'. Finish off by clicking the Stop Recording symbol (the solid square on the Stop recording dialogue box). If all's well clicking on the new toolbar button will place the text wherever the cursor is flashing. The same basic technique can be used to automate almost any action: have a go, it's not difficult!

Using Wordbasic

This second example is based on WordBasic commands and it will automatically save a Word document to the hard disk and make a backup to floppy disk. Give it a try –, it only takes a few minutes to key in. It's fairly rudimentary and assumes your hard disk is drive C: and you're backing up to a floppy in drive A:.

Begin with a blank open document in Word. From the Tools menu select Macro, then Macros; give it a name and click on the Create button. The WordBasic window opens and you will see a flashing cursor after the word 'Sub', (and before the word End Sub). Type in the following text, carefully observing the syntax and all of the line breaks.

```
Dim strName$
Dim ch
WordBasic.FileSave
strName$ = WordBasic.[Filename$](1)
ch = Len(strName$) - 1
While Mid(strName$, ch, 1) <> "\" And Mid(strName$, ch, 1) <> ":"
ch = ch - 1
Wend
strName$ = Mid(strName$, ch + 1)
WordBasic.PrintStatusBar "Backing Up" + WordBasic.[Filename$](1) +
" To " + Ini$ + strName$
WordBasic.CopyFile WordBasic.[Filename$](1), "A:\" + strName$
WordBasic.MsgBox "Boot Up Backup Complete"
```

You can now assign the macro a button on the toolbar (or keyboard shortcut). Click on Customize on the Tools menu, select the Commands tab, scroll down the list in the left hand window and click on Macros. Drag and drop your new macro onto a toolbar. Select an icon using the same procedure for macro recording (see earlier).

HOME INCOME CALCULATOR

A spreadsheet is basically a smart calculator – the classic number-crunching program. They're aptly described as word processors for numbers, and they can be just as useful. The suite of bundled software that came with your PC almost certainly included a spreadsheet, the best known being Lotus 1-2-3, Microsoft Excel and Claris Works. As we have shown, there are also simple spreadsheet functions in word processors plus plenty of freeware and shareware programs available for the cost of a download on the Internet, so you have no excuse not to get to know this incredibly versatile application.

The best way to do that is to use one. We're going to show you how to create a simple home income calculator. The same basic techniques can be used to track the finances of a small business, club or society, generate a price list or even help to navigate an aircraft or boat – in fact, any application where numbers interact with each other. Spreadsheets do not depend on the latest super-fast processor chips or bucket-loads of memory, and once you've become familiar with the basics you can quickly adapt to using any spreadsheet on any

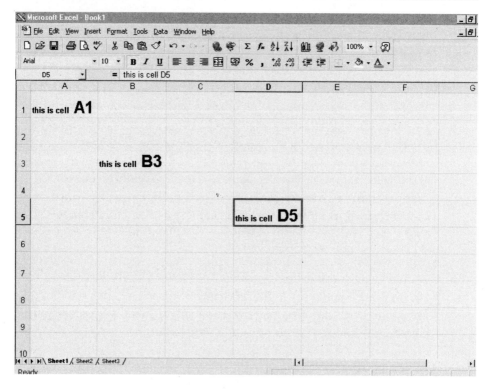

Cells in a spreadsheet or table are designated using a simple code

computer, from a Sinclair Spectrum to an Apple iMac.

In this example we'll be using MS Excel; it is included in the Office and Works software suites and also sold separately. By sheer weight of numbers it is the one you're most likely to have; however, the procedures in this example will work with almost any other spreadsheet program and can easily be adapted to work with the table functions in MS Word.

The first thing you see when you open a spreadsheet program will be a blank table or grid. By convention vertical columns are labelled alphabetically, and rows numerically. By this means every square or 'cell' on the table has a unique identity code, i.e. the square in the top left hand corner is A1, the one next to its right is B1, and so on. Begin by typing in the months of the year along the top row, starting in cell B1. Excel has a neat little trick to save you the effort of keying text or numbers that follow a logical sequence. When you've typed in the first month move the mouse pointer to the bottom right-hand corner of the cell, where it changes to a black plus sign. Click and hold then drag the pointer along row 1, as it passes each column you'll see the month change. Stop when you come to M1 and a whole year's worth of correctly ordered months will be entered into the cells.

Now enter some expenditure headings into column A. You might want to make the column a tad wider to accommodate a line of text. In Excel put the mouse pointer into the shaded row of letters at the top and on to a column line, click hold and move the line slightly to the right. Obviously our headings as shown in the diagram are only a suggestion – put in as many or as few as you think necessary. When you have finished skip a row and put in something like 'Total Outgoings'. In the cell underneath – A15 in our case – type 'Income', and below that, in A16, 'What's Left'.

At this point you can begin to key in some figures. If any of your outgoings are fixed – such as your mortgage, or any other standing orders

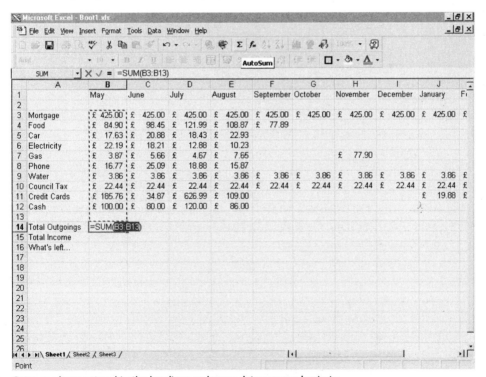

Once you have entered in the headings and some data you can begin to assign formulas to the cells

– type them in just once and use the logical sequence trick outlined above. This time it will repeat the same figure in each cell in a row. You can assign a pound sign to all of the cells containing numbers in Excel by highlighting the whole table in the same way you highlight a block of text in a word processor. Put the mouse pointer into the top-left corner, click hold and drop in the bottom-right corner, then on the toolbar click on the currency icon (a banknote and coins).

When you have entered all of the information click and highlight cell B14 (or whichever one relates to your Total Outgoings for the first month) and click on the AutoSum button on the Toolbar (shaped like a Greek letter E). This adds together all of the numbers in the column above. Another way of doing that is to manually assign a mathematical expression to that cell. Click on the cell and type in '=SUM (B3:B12)'. You're telling the spreadsheet to add together or sum all of the numbers in cells B3 to B12. This formula has to be inserted into every column in row 14, but again in Excel it is possible to do this in one step

	A	B	C	D	E	F	G	H	I	J	Fi
1		May	June	July	August	September	October	November	December	January	
2											
3	Mortgage	£ 425.00	£ 425.00	£ 425.00	£ 425.00	£ 425.00	£ 425.00	£ 425.00	£ 425.00	£ 425.00	£
4	Food	£ 84.90	£ 98.45	£ 121.99	£ 108.87	£ 77.89					
5	Car	£ 17.63	£ 20.88	£ 18.43	£ 22.93						
6	Electricity	£ 22.19	£ 18.21	£ 12.88	£ 10.23						
7	Gas	£ 3.87	£ 5.66	£ 4.67	£ 7.65			£ 77.90			
8	Phone	£ 16.77	£ 25.09	£ 18.88	£ 15.87						
9	Water	£ 3.86	£ 3.86	£ 3.86	£ 3.86	£ 3.86	£ 3.86	£ 3.86	£ 3.86	£ 3.86	£
10	Council Tax	£ 22.44	£ 22.44	£ 22.44	£ 22.44	£ 22.44	£ 22.44	£ 22.44	£ 22.44	£ 22.44	£
11	Credit Cards	£ 185.76	£ 34.87	£ 626.99	£ 109.00					£ 19.88	£
12	Cash	£ 100.00	£ 80.00	£ 120.00	£ 86.00						
13											
14	Total Outgoings	£ 882.42	£ 734.46	£1,375.14	£ 811.85	£ 529.19	£ 451.30	£ 529.20	£ 451.30	£ 471.18	£
15	Total Income	£1,100.00	£1,100.00	£1,100.00	£1,100.00	£1,100.00	£1,100.00	£1,100.00	£1,100.00	£1,100.00	£
16	What's left...	£ 217.58	£ 365.54	-£ 275.14	£ 288.15	£ 570.81	£ 648.70	£ 570.80	£ 648.70	£ 628.82	£

Calculations are carried out automatically as you enter figures into the columns

by clicking in the bottom right-hand corner of the cell and dragging it along the row. Excel automatically changes the column letter as it goes.

Finally, in cell B16, 'What's Left', insert the expression B15-B14; this subtracts the total outgoings in B14 from the income in B15, to show how much is left. Repeat the formula in the relevant cells along the row as before. The spreadsheet is now complete and all calculations are carried out automatically as you type in or change figures.

If you like you can instruct Excel to show negative numbers – i.e. when your outgoings exceed your income – in red. On the Format menu, click on Cells and select the Number tab and, click on Number in the Category window and highlight the red-coloured '-1234.10' entry in the negative numbers panel. The 'Cells' option on the Format menu also has the facility to add colours and shading to rows columns or blocks within the table – you'll find it on the Patterns tab, highlight the area you want to stand out first and choose a colour.

Q&A **Real world problems**

Excel-ent idea?

Q   I have a small but slightly irritating problem with Microsoft Excel 97. Every time I try to enter a lower case 'i' in a cell (with no other text in the cell) it immediately changes to upper case when I press enter. This happens with all font types. I realise that this is hardly an earth-shattering problem but now that I've noticed it, I wonder why it does it and how I can stop it. Is this a deliberate bug put in as a joke by the people who compiled Excel to see how long it would take to be noticed?
T. M. *via e-mail*

A   Changing lower case i to uppercase is a supposedly helpful 'Auto-Correct' action. It can be disabled by clicking on AutoCorrect on the Tools menu. Scroll down the list, highlight the 'Replace 'i' with ... entry and click Delete. Alternatively, uncheck the box marked 'Replace text as you type' to switch off AutoCorrect altogether.

Coy calc

Q   I have Windows 98 and the other day wanted to use the Windows calculator that I had used, occasionally, in both Windows 95 and Windows 3.1, but couldn't find it. Has it been dropped or is it simply hidden? I would value your help in re-locating it or can you tell me where I can find a simple calculator on the Internet.
M. K. via e-mail

A   The Calculator is included in Windows 98. It normally resides in Start > Programs > Accessories, but it sounds as though yours wasn't loaded when your operating system was installed. To put it on to your system you will need your original Windows 98 CD-ROM. Open Control Panel (Start > Settings), click on Add/Remove Programs, select the Windows Setup tab, double click the Accessories icon, put a tick next to Calculator and follow the instructions.

By the way, there are hundreds of freeware and shareware calculators on the Internet, covering just about every application you care to name (biorhythms, golf handicap, Euro currency conversion, time and distance, scientific etc.) you'll find a huge selection at www.download. com, just type 'calculators' in the Search field.

Unfriendly words?

Q   My local PC dealer offers two software packages with his machines. Pack A contains Windows 98 and Lotus SmartSuite while Pack B contains Windows 98 and Microsoft Office 97 (Small Business Edition). I need to handle documents and tables in both Lotus and Microsoft formats, so I enquired as to the possibility of purchasing both suites, but only one copy of Windows 98. I was told that it is not possible to install both together. Is this correct?
P. F. via e-mail

A   Piffle! Office and SmartSuite can coexist on the same PC, though you may not need to bother as MS Word can read WordPro document files and vice-versa.

CHAPTER 4 **Pictures and images**

Your Windows PC is a powerful image manipulation tool. All the software is there, you just need to know where to find it.

Computers have been doing all sorts of useful things with words and numbers since day one but only recently have they been able to handle graphics and complex images. It began back in the late 1980s, following the launch of the 386 family of microprocessors and version 3 of the Windows operating system. However, PCs and pictures really got going with the development of the Pentium processor, cheaper memory chips, bigger disk drives and Windows 95 and 98.

A good way to learn about your PC's image processing abilities is a frequently overlooked utility in Windows called Microsoft Paint. You may have come across Paint already; if not, you will find it by clicking on the Start button, then Programs and it should be in the Accessories folder. Double click the Paint icon and if the desktop doesn't fill the screen use the maximise button (next to the Close button) to expand the window. Make sure the Tool Box and Colour Box options are enabled on the View menu. By the way, most versions of Paint are broadly similar though the one included in Windows 98 has a few extra bells and whistles, including the ability to work with compressed JPEG images. Earlier versions included with Windows 3.x and Windows 95 are limited to bitmap (*.bmp) and PCX (*.pcx) files. The best way to get to know Paint and what it can do is to play around with it.

Start by drawing a few squiggles with the paintbrush, experiment with different brush sizes and colours. It's easy to draw lines and shapes using the various tools. Try the paint can, this is used to fill in an area with colour, the airbrush can be used to give subtle shades and the eye-dropper picks up a colour from any area of the picture, for drawing or painting. Notice that if you click on the letter 'A' in the

Toolbox a re-sizeable box appears on the screen, into which you can type text. A dialogue box appears that allows you to choose the type-face and font size. Now try editing your image, the eraser is especially useful. For really precise changes use the zoom facility, at the highest magnification levels you can easily change a single pixel.

Projects

CREATING YOUR SIGNATURE

Now it's time to put those new-found skills into practice and do some-thing useful with Paint. Here's how to turn your signature into an image file. Writing with a mouse is difficult, so draw a large version of your signature on a sheet of paper and trace it with the mouse, using a simple pointer – a matchstick or cocktail stick – stuck to the mouse with some sticky tape will do the trick. When you're happy with it give the image file a name and save it. Now use the rectangular Copy tool to put a dotted box around it, then copy it to the clipboard using Ctrl + C or the Copy function on the Edit menu. Now you can add your sig-nature to a fax cover page, or a standard letter template by pasting the image (Ctrl + V, or Paste on the Edit menu) into the open document. Once it is in place use the mouse to re-size the image by clicking on the corners of the outline box.

You can use Paint to create a simple logo or letterhead design, and don't forget the facility to include text in your design. When you've fin-ished, make sure you name and save the file somewhere you can easily find it.

CUSTOMISING WINDOWS SCREENS

Paint can be used to change the annoying 'Please wait ....' and 'It is now safe ....' shutdown screens that appear whenever you exit Win-dows. The same techniques can also be used to modify or even create your own opening and closing screens.

The two Windows closing screens live in files called logo.sys and

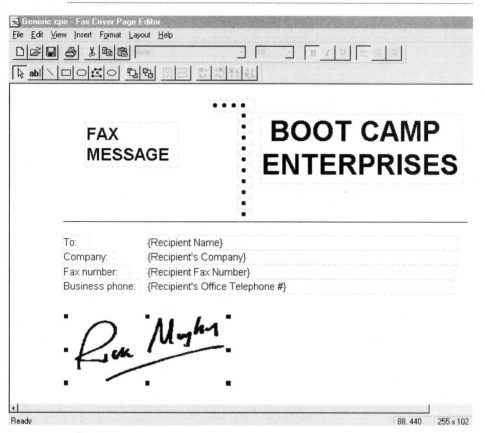

Once you have created an image file of your signature you can enter it into documents and fax cover sheets

logow.sys and they are stored in the main Windows directory on the C: drive. The opening Windows 95 and 98 clouds screen is called logo.sys and it too lives in the Windows folder, though on some PCs it may end up embedded in a file called io.sys, and you won't be able to get at it using Paint. However, any suitable image file, with the name logo.sys, placed in the root of the C: drive will override the original clouds image, but more about what that entails in a moment.

The first thing you must do is rename the original image files, otherwise you won't be able to restore them, should you ever wish to do so. Open Windows Explorer, find the picture file you're going to work on and either right click and use the rename option, or left click on the file icon to highlight it, wait a second and click again to activate the name field. Change the .sys extension to .old or something similar. Now back to Paint, open the image file and immediately rename it with its original .sys extension, using the Save As command.

You will notice that the image looks a bit odd; it's squeezed horizontally into a 320 × 400 pixel shape, but it assumes its correct proportions when shown by Windows. Now you can do whatever you like with it. Have a doodle, add your own witty message, use the paintbrush, fill can or airbrush. You can erase or change the shape of the clouds by picking up the blue or white colour with the eyedropper and using a paintbrush or airbrush.

Why not create your own opening or closing screen from scratch? That's easy too. The only points to bear in mind are that any image must be saved as a 256-colour 320 × 400-pixel bitmap. You will find the latter option on the Image menu, under Attributes; the 256-colour designation is on the Save As window listed under 'File As Type'. The

You can design or create your own Windows screen using Windows
Paint, but watch the size settings

same parameters must also be applied to any other image you want to use as an opening or closing screen. You can use photographs but you will find that the limited number of colours makes it look a bit messy – it works best with simple images and designs, but the point is you decide. Have a go; it's very liberating, putting you back in charge of Windows!

ADVANCED GRAPHICS

Paint is a useful little program but it has its limits. In order to unleash the image processing potential of your PC you will need something a little more sophisticated.

PaintShop Pro fits the bill very neatly; it is the visual equivalent of a word processor or spreadsheet, able to do quite extraordinary things to pictures and photographs, that just a few years ago would have been possible only in a well-equipped photo studio or processing lab-

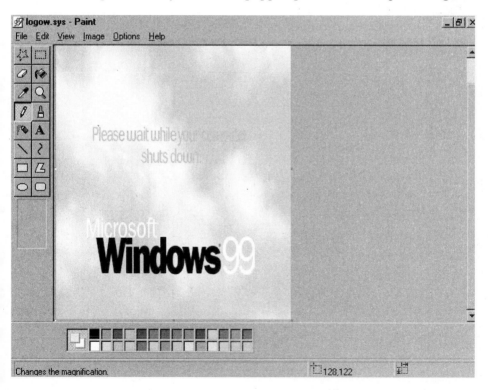

Don't worry if the proportions look wrong, the shape will be correct when it is displayed

oratory. PaintShop Pro – known as PSP to its many friends and admirers – is by no means the most powerful or advanced 'paint box' program on the market, but it is very easy to use, and it is cheap (the current version costs around £80). In fact you can try it for free as shareware versions are regularly featured on computer magazine CD-ROMs and it can be downloaded from the Internet (www.jasc.com).

One of PSP's key features is the vast number of image file formats it can handle – more than 40 of them in the case of the current version 5. That means it can display and convert images for a wide range of applications, but it is the huge range of tools and effects that will be of interest to most users. We'll begin by using just a couple of them to fix one of the commonest photographic problems: red-eye. Later on we'll show you how to use PSP to edit a photograph and remove an unwanted object or person from a picture.

REMOVING RED-EYE

Red-eye is caused by a reflection of camera flash; it gives the subject a devilish appearance and can ruin an otherwise perfectly good photograph that you want to use in a document, or send to a friend or relative via e-mail. Step one is to import the picture into PSP, either by scanning, or by reading the image file, if it was shot on an electronic still camera or downloaded from the Internet. Once on the page you can correct any exposure and colour errors. The Adjust option on the Colours menu contains sliders for varying brightness and contrast, plus more subtle adjustments to highlights, gamma correction, midtones, shadows, hues, colour saturation and balance.

Next, use the magnification tool (magnifying glass icon) to enlarge the section of the image containing the eyes to a manageable size. The magnification factor can be increased or decreased using the left and right mouse buttons. Now, using the Freehand Selection tool (shaped like a lasso), carefully outline the red pupil. From the Colours menu select Adjust and the Hue, Saturation and Luminance (Lightness on PSP 5) option. Use the saturation control to reduce the depth of the colour in the outlined area (–100 on the dialogue box). This removes the red colour but doesn't affect details, like reflections, so it looks completely natural. Repeat the process on the other eye and save the image file.

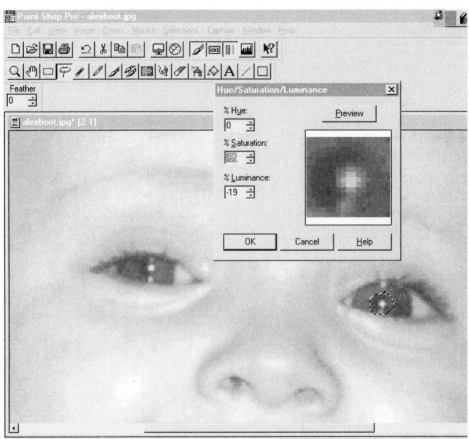

Use the hue and luminance tools to eliminate red-eye in photographs

You can also use this opportunity to try out another of PSP's clever tools and remove blemishes, spots and pimples or other unwanted details, like straggly hairs. If necessary, increase the magnification to centre the blemish on the screen. Select the Clone Brush icon (two paintbrushes) and position it to one side of the area you wish to mask. Click the right mouse button and it picks up the colour and texture of a small area beneath the brush – shown by a set of cross-hairs. Now use the right button to 'spray' the recorded detail into the blemish. With a little practice it is possible to make completely invisible alterations.

The copy tool can be used to replicate parts of the background

EDITING AN IMAGE

PSP has a variety of tools for removing or hiding larger objects, including people. The cloning brush is fine for smaller details, but it can be difficult to accurately simulate more complex backgrounds and textures. The solution is to copy and paste sections of the background and use them to cover up the object. Select an area to copy using the freehand tool, PSP has a 'feather' facility that blurs the edges of the selected area, so that it blends in more easily with its surroundings (a dialogue box will appear, choose a setting of between 10 and 15). Go to the Selections menu and click on 'Float', this copies the selected area; if you forget to select Float you will leave a hole behind when you move the patch of picture. Use the mouse to position it over the subject. If the background is very uneven – plants, trees etc. – then you may find it

You can easily make people or objects disappear from your photographs

looks better if you do it in small irregularly sized chunks, to give it a more natural appearance. At this stage don't worry too much about rough or uneven edges, you can tidy it up afterwards with the clone brush or the retouch mode (hand icon) which will blur and soften details.

We've barely scratched the surface of what PSP can do, just describing what the special effects can do would fill several chapters but the really good thing about this program is that it is highly intuitive and very easy to get to know, simply by using it. Try it, and if you continue to use the shareware version beyond the 30-day trial period – and you probably will – don't forget to register and pay for it.

Q&A   **Real world problems**

Screen test

Q   I note that a lot of books and magazines show Windows screen displays as pictures. Can you tell me what software to use to capture the screen display as a file, which can be incorporated in a DTP file? I would also like to know the source of the program.
J. L. via e-mail

A   Windows contains everything you need to insert a 'screen grab' into a document. Simply press the PrtScn button on your keyboard and a snapshot or 'bitmap' of whatever is on the screen is sent to the Windows Clipboard. From there it can be opened and manipulated using the Paint program, or pasted into a document using the Paste command. If you only want to capture the 'active' window in a display then hold down the Alt key before pressing Print Screen button. If you want to do anything more complicated with the image then you will need a graphics program, such as Paint Shop Pro.

Paint potty

Q   My children have been playing with the Paint program on my PC and have somehow managed to drag the ToolBox off the screen. How do I get it back? It does not return when using the View Command.
M. A. Hants

A   You have to be quite determined to make a tool boxes or menu bars disappear, but it can be done … Although the box appears to have vanished from the screen it can normally be recovered. Make sure ToolBox is checked in the View menu then maximise the Paint Window. Use the mouse pointer to probe the edges of the display, clicking the left mouse button as you do so. Sooner or later you'll discover a vestige of the ToolBox – it may just be a short white line – but it will highlight when you click the mouse. When you find it you can either drag it back onto the desktop or fast click on the edge of the box several times and this will put it back in its place.

Image consultant

Q I have downloaded some images, which are in JPEG format. Is it pos-
sible to find out the dimensions of these images before printing them?
Also, can JPEG images be scaled up or down? I have tried opening a
JPEG image file in Paint but get the message that the program has per-
formed an illegal operation and will be closed down.
T. C. via e-mail

A The short answer to all of your questions is yes, but in order to analyse
and manipulate a JPEG image you will need something a little more
sophisticated than Paint. There are now many excellent programs to
choose from including powerful packages such as Adobe PhotoShop,
Corel Draw, MGI PhotoSuite, Microsoft Picture It Serif Design Studio,
to name just a few.

Custom clock

Q How can I create my own screensaver? It struck me that it would be
very useful to have an analogue clock ticking away on the screen when
it has gone into the save mode. I thought it would just be a simple
matter of dropping Clock.exe into one of the screensavers in Windows
System, but it ain't that easy! The trouble is that your regular, sometimes deceptively simple, answers to complex questions have encour-
aged me to think that I could do it myself. It's a classic case of 'a little
knowledge is a dangerous thing'.
D. C. via e-mail

A Well, it was worth a try … Fortunately there's a much easier way and
that's to download one of the dozens of freeware and shareware programs from the Internet. A quick search on Yahoo using Clock and
Screensaver as keywords brought up a couple of dozen sites. There's
an interesting selection at http://traknet.softseek.com/Desktop_
Enhancements/Screen_Savers/Clocks_and_Countdowns. This assortment includes a 'death' clock (you tell it how old you are and your sex
and it tells you how long you have left to live …). There's also a cus-
tomisable screensaver with a clock at http://ftp.pcworld.com/pub/
desktop/screen_savers/phantastic.exe.

Screen clean

Q I have downloaded screensavers from Internet web sites but they need updating. How do I remove the old to make room for new?
D.B. via e-mail

A Why do you want to remove them? You can change screensavers and settings from the Display icon in Control Panel (Start then Settings). Most screensaver files are quite small and deleting them probably won't regain you much hard disk space. Leave them alone and they won't bother you, but if you insist on going ahead with the cull then you will find most of them lurking in the 'System' folder, inside your Windows program. They have the extension .scr and usually – though not always – have a small monitor icon next to the listing. Alternatively open Find on the Start menu and type *.scr then click on Find Now, and it should list all of the screensavers on your system. Do not remove files willy-nilly and be aware that not all files with the extension .scr are screensavers. Whenever you delete a file from an important folder like Windows System wait for a day or two before emptying the Recycle Bin; if there is a problem, you can always restore the file. Some more elaborate screensavers may live in their own separate folders, in which case use the program's uninstall utility – if provided – or Add/Remove Programs in Control panel.

Handy scanner

Q I've been using my scanner to scan my baby's hands and feet, which seems a marvellous method, and prevents getting paint on the child's hands. However, I cannot get a 1:1 scaled image. Even if I put the scanner into photocopy mode, the printout is a little smaller than the original. How can I print out full size image?
D. P. via e-mail

A It is not unusual for scanned and photocopied images to be a slightly different size to the original. There should be a way of compensating for this in your chosen (or supplied) paint-box/graphics software, usually under the print preview menu. Most programs have a sizing facility to alter the dimensions of the image as it is printed. You can easily calibrate your set-up by scanning a small ruler, print it out and adjust the image size accordingly.

Picture this

Q   Having recently acquired a scanner I wonder if you can tell me if it is possible to create CD-ROMs of my colour photos? I have a Pentium MMX 166 running Windows 95 and an Epson colour printer.
C. A. via e-mail

A   You don't even need a scanner: a lot of high street photo processors will record your 35 mm photographs on to Kodak Photo CD discs, that can be read on almost any CD-ROM drive (with suitable software). You can find out more from the Kodak web site at http://www.kodak.co.uk.

If you want to do it yourself, then you will need a recordable CD-ROM drive; prices start at under £200 (see Chapter 10). Home-made CD-ROM picture disks can be played on any PC, though again some additional software may be needed, depending on the file formats used.

Prints of darkness

Q   I have recently bought a scanner; it seems to work well, if a little slowly but we have problems printing the results. The main difficulty concerns watercolour paintings that we are trying to print out. They scan well, if the results on the screen are anything to go by, but when they are printed the colours are dark and harsh. I am using a HP DeskJet 600 with a colour cartridge. The very helpful chap in the local computer shop suggested altering the printer settings, but to no avail. Any help, in words of one syllable that could be understood by a middle-aged home computer user would be most welcome.

One other question: what is the light fastness of colour prints and do different models produce varying results?
K. P. via e-mail

A   The paint or graphics software that came with your scanner should allow you to alter basic colour and brightness settings; if not, then it's worth changing to a more advanced program. Your monitor might be giving a false impression; make sure it is set up correctly and the type of paper you are using can also affect print quality. For best results use high-quality, low absorbency grades, specifically designed for inkjet printing.

Most inkjet printers use water-based inks and these will begin to fade after only a few years, faster if the print is exposed to bright light or stored in a humid atmosphere. Longer lasting UV stabilised inks are available for HP and other makes of printer that should last 25 years or more.

Wasteful saver?

Q   My sister recently told me that using a screen saver tied up a lot of RAM. Is that the case? If so are they really necessary or just a gimmick and do they use up that memory even when they are not in use because you are utilising the keyboard or the mouse. Is the potential damage to your screen overstated and does the same potential exist for the new flat screens? When downloading from the net, should the screen saver be turned off first to conserve memory and hopefully speed up the process? *D. A. via e-mail*

A   Screen savers only use memory resources when they are actually running, which is not a problem since the PC is idle. Windows power management schemes have made screen-burn much less of a problem, but it can still happen if a bright static image is left on the screen for hours on end; however, this doesn't affect flat panel LCD screens. Disabling your screen saver won't make a jot of difference to Internet download times.

CHAPTER 5 **Getting on the net**

The impact the Internet will have on our lives has been likened to the Industrial Revolution; that could be an understatement.

Ignore the hype and jargon, the Internet is simply a very useful thing to have; moreover, it's fun, informative and very easy to use. If you haven't yet seen what it can do and still need convincing ask anyone who has been using it for more than a couple of weeks for a demonstration. You probably won't have to look very far: there are over ten million Internet users in the UK right now, with tens of thousands more signing up each week. So where do you begin?

Doubtless one day you will be able to 'surf' the net from the comfort of your armchair, on your living room TV, via a cheap black box. However, for the moment the only sensible option – if you want to do the job properly – is to have a PC and a telephone line. (It is possible to use a mobile phone but it is painfully slow and horrendously expensive).

The PC doesn't need to be anything special; virtually any model made within the last five years will do, but fairly recent multimedia models (Windows, IBM PC/compatible or Mac) are easiest to use. The PC will need to be connected to or fitted with a device called a modem (more or less standard these days) that allows it to communicate over the telephone network, and you will need to sign up with an Internet Service Provider or ISP.

An ISP is a company that provides you with a gateway onto the Internet via their 'server' computer. The ISP will supply you with an e-mail address and mailbox, where messages sent to you are stored; these days many ISPs also throw in several megabytes of space on their server computer for personal web sites. Some ISPs, known as content providers, maintain their own extensive web sites, usually for the exclusive use of their customers. They're packed with extra services (news, sports, travel, shopping, on-line banking etc.) and they may act as hosts to newsgroups and so-called 'communities'. These are specialised Internet sites where like-minded users can meet and exchange ideas.

Once you have the PC and a telephone it need cost only a few pennies a day to use the Internet. One expense you can't avoid is the cost of connecting to the ISP by telephone. Some telephone companies do offer free calls at certain times but telephone charges of one sort or another are unavoidable. However, most ISPs use local numbers or a special line charged at local rates, costing from a penny or so a minute off-peak and at weekends. That stays the same even if the Internet site you are connected to is 200 hundred yards down the road or on "the other side of the world. The same applies to sending and receiving e-mail messages.

Internet access software or 'browsers' are normally supplied free; you may already have one or more installed on your PC. They are also widely distributed on magazine cover-mount CD-ROMs, and one will be sent to you when you contact the ISP. A few service providers still impose a one-off set-up charge and some still require a monthly subscription; however, the majority of ISPs now offer a completely free access. They make their money from advertising or they receive a slice of the income from the BT lines used by their customers. In some cases they may also charge heavily for technical support (up to £1 a minute) and you will probably end up with advertising banners and logos appearing on your computer screen.

Fears that free ISPs might fail, be unable to cope with the demand or offer a second-class service have proved largely unfounded, but it remains a consideration, particularly if you require a reliable Internet connection for business or commercial use. The longer established broad-based companies and specialist providers may also offer more overseas connections or 'points of presence' (POP) that you can dial up when you are abroad, to collect your e-mail.

With so many ISPs to choose from (there are almost 300 of them in the UK) it can be very difficult but there's nothing to stop you playing the field before you make up your mind. Most of the well-known, pay-to-use ISPs offer no-obligation 30-day free trials. They will ask you to give them your credit card details, so remember to cancel well before the trial period expires if you do not intend to go on using it. Most Internet access software is supplied on CD-ROM and installation is normally quite straightforward: pop in the disk and follow the instructions. Occasionally something goes wrong, so if you are a complete novice ask a knowledgeable friend to be on hand and it's a good idea to have an 'uninstaller' program on your PC (for example, CleanSweep or Uninstaller). Try just one service at a time – some access software can disagree with other programs – and remember to thoroughly erase unused programs.

BROWSERS

If you've decided to get connected to the Internet one of the first things you have to do is get to grips with a program called a browser. The browser's job is to open a window onto the Internet by translating data coming down the telephone line into a form that can be processed and displayed on a PC. The browser helps you to find your way around the Internet and locate web sites, by typing in those odd-looking addresses or URLs that begin with 'http' and 'www'. A browser is also a gateway for e-mail and, if required, it will store messages, act as an address book and list 'bookmarks' for frequently accessed or 'favourite' web sites.

Browsers have become one of the bogeymen of the PC world and they are probably responsible for more problems than all other types of programs put together. They cause crashes, squabble with other types of software and behave in mysterious ways that can make a PC user's life an absolute misery. You may well be lucky and get on-line and onto the net without any problems, but find some wood and touch it fast! Trust me, your time will come.

That time will come sooner rather than later if you fiddle around with your browser's critical settings, and there are plenty of them, tucked away on the various menus. That is not to say you shouldn't configure your PC to work the way you want it to; however, be patient, especially if you are new to PCs, Windows or the Internet.

Before you touch anything, get to know your enemy. Browsers fall into two basic categories. Internet Access Providers (IAPs) such as Cable & Wireless, Pipex etc., who supply only basic Internet and e-mail facilities, generally use one of the two most popular browsers, Netscape or Internet Explorer. Internet Explorer version 3 (IE3) was included with Windows 95. Internet Explorer 4 (IE4) appeared with later releases of Windows 95 and it is an integral component of Windows 98 and Internet Explorer 5 (IE5) is now supplied by most ISPs. Netscape Navigator (version 3) and the recently released Netscape Communicator are also loaded on most new PCs as a matter of course.

The second type of browser is a customised version of Internet Explorer (occasionally Netscape Navigator). These are mostly supplied by the older well-established ISPs such as AOL and CompuServe that have their own unique content (on-line shopping, news, sports, travel, forums etc.). Free access ISPs also tend to customise their browsers with banners, logos and watermarks, but the basic layout, appearance and functions are normally unchanged.

When you sign up for Internet access the browser software is automatically installed or configured on your PC, and at that stage you have little say in the matter. However, there is no reason why you have to put up with it. You may well want to change, particularly if you find you don't get on with the supplied browser or you are used to another program. There are quite significant differences in the way browsers operate and perform. Some make it easier than others to find and display Internet pages; e-mail facilities also differ widely and you may not want all of the extra bumf or advertising that comes with a custom program. You might even want to use two different browsers – one for e-mail, the other for the net – either way, making the change is not too difficult.

It is better to do this kind of thing quite early on as some browsers – especially the custom versions – can make it difficult or even impossible to transfer address books and bookmarks to other programs. After only a few weeks on the Internet these lists can grow quite large. We'll look at the two most common scenarios: changing the default browser on your PC, and replacing a custom browser with Netscape or Internet Explorer.

Projects

CHANGING YOUR BROWSER

If your current browser is Internet Explorer (version 3x, 4x or 5x) and
you want to switch to Netscape, open Internet Explorer (stay off-line),
go to the View menu and click on Internet Options. Select the Programs
tab, at the bottom of the dialogue box there is a tick-box marked 'Internet Explorer should check to see whether it is the default browser'.

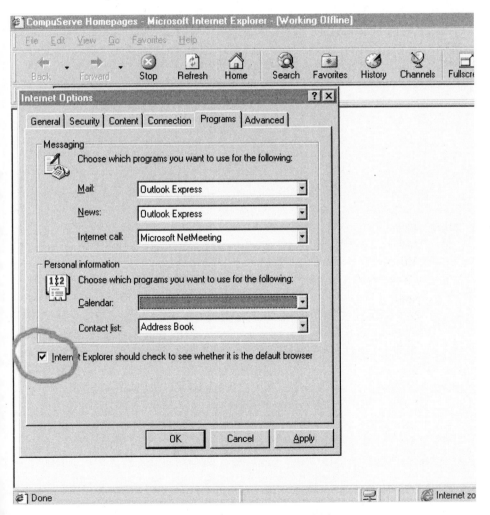

You can make Internet Explorer your default browser by checking this box

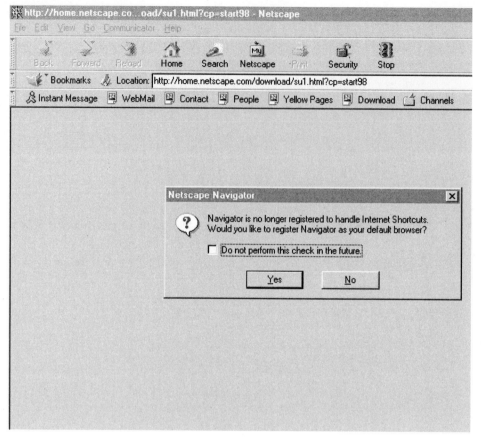

If you change browsers you will see a message box like this to confirm
your action

Uncheck the box and the next time you start Netscape it will ask you if
you want to make it your default browser, click OK and it's done.

To use Netscape or Internet Explorer instead of the one provided by
CompuServe, say, click on My Computer and open Dial-Up Networking. There you will find at least two icons, one for creating new connections the other one for your current ISP connection. Click on it and
enter the requested password and user name information. You will
need to re-configure the mailbox in CompuServe as it uses a propri-
etary e-mail system. If you want to use your new browser to pick up
CompuServe mail it has to be changed to the more common 'POP3'
protocol. It's not difficult but once the change has been made you

won't be able to alter your e-mail address or user name. POP3 can be switched on during a CompuServe session (Go popmail) but it's a good idea to read the FAQ first (Go UKHF, Files > Sending e-mail > POP3 Services). AOL's highly modified Internet Explorer browser is truly horrible. The simplest solution is to log on and then run plain vanilla Navigator or Internet Explorer over the top of it; you will, however, still have to use the AOL browser for e-mail.

SECURITY ON THE NET

How secure is the Internet? The simple answer is that it isn't, and everything you read, write, see, hear or say via your PC can be monitored and recorded by anyone with a mind to do so. The Internet is also the main distribution channel for computer viruses and on-line fraud has the potential to become a major problem.

But let's not get paranoid, the Internet is no more vulnerable to snooping and chicanery than a telephone or what comes through your letterbox. Here's another comforting thought: the size, complexity and sheer amount of traffic on the Internet has made casual eavesdropping that much more difficult and less likely that anyone would be interested in what you get up to, unless you are handling sensitive material, or up to no good. Nevertheless, for anyone buying products or services on-line or if you simply want your business to remain private then security, or rather the lack of it, remains an issue.

The weakest link in the whole chain is your PC, though fears that an Internet connection will make it possible for others to 'hack' into your computer are largely groundless. Unless your stand-alone Windows PC is specifically configured for networking or file sharing there is little or no chance of anyone remotely accessing or interfering with your machine. If they can get to your computer by other means, that's a different story. Your PC's hard disk holds a wealth of information about what you have been up to on the Internet, as well as copies of all of your incoming and outgoing e-mails.

Internet browsers have what are known as 'caches' and history folders that store web site addresses plus copies of the pages, pictures and documents you have viewed. There's nothing sinister in this; their job is to help you find previously visited web sites and speed up downloads. Caches may also contain small files called 'cookies' planted in your PC by web sites. They are mostly harmless and contain information that the web site uses to tailor a page to suit your browser software or personal preferences. Nevertheless they provide an easy to follow paper-trail of where you've been and what you've been looking at. If that is a concern then you should take control of your browser's cache and history files. History and the Internet Explorer cache can both be found inside the Windows directory; Navigator's cache is in the Netscape directory.

COVERING YOUR TRACKS

You can safely delete any of the files in the cache manually from Windows Explorer and as a bonus recover some hard disk space, but be warned that this is not a complete solution and 'ghost' files are left behind that can be found relatively easily. Erasing browser cache files from within DOS is a good first-level defence though the 'deltree' command should be used only by those who know their way around MS-DOS and again there are ways and means of recovering deleted files that only specialised software can defeat.

Internet Explorer has a facility to limit the size of the cache and clear the history folder; both can be found under Internet Options on the View menu. On the General tab set 'Days to Keep History' to zero, and on the Settings button under Temporary Internet Files set the slider to minimum. There are also a number of software utilities that will automatically clear browser cache and history folders; the best known is the 'Paranoia' tool in Tweak UI. Tweak UI is Freeware and is included on the Windows 98 CD-ROM or it can be downloaded from the Microsoft web site (www.microsoft.com).

KEEP IT PRIVATE

There is only one sure way to protect e-mails and text files stored on your PC and that is to encrypt them so they cannot be read. Encryption is also the only means to prevent others from reading your messages when they are sent over the Internet, and remember your e-mail could pass through dozens of other computers in many different countries during its journey. Powerful encryption software is readily available in the Internet; one of the best places to start is the Tucows web site (http://tucows.ukonline.co.uk), which contains more than a score of freeware and shareware utilities. This includes the 'international' version PGP, or Pretty Good Privacy, which is generally reckoned to be one of the most powerful encryption programs available, so powerful in fact that the American government classifies it as munitions and have gone to considerable lengths to prevent its distribution outside the USA. The Tucows site also has some useful file hiding and deletion utilities and cookie zappers, so it is well worth a visit.

On-line shopping and banking has generated a lot of scary headlines but the truth is the risk of fraud need be no greater than buying goods on the phone with your credit card, provided you take a few sensible precautions. Rule number one is to keep your wits about you and avoid dealing with shady-sounding companies in distant lands. If the products or services they are selling seem too cheap to be true, they probably are! Web sites with well-signposted security features, such as passwords and secure/encrypted transmission systems inspire a certain amount of confidence, and always keep a printout of the order page or form. Credit cards are the safest payment method and card companies provide their customers with protection against fraud. Beware of hidden charges when buying from overseas web sites. In addition to carriage costs you will almost certainly have to pay UK import duty and VAT on your purchases, and this may well wipe out any savings you might have made on the cost.

Finally, a few words about downloading files from the Internet. Destructive viruses lurking in e-mail attachments and programs are not that common, but it pays to be vigilant. Plain text e-mails are safe to open and read but everything else should be treated as suspect and pass through your virus checker (you have got one, haven't you? If not, you are just asking for trouble). It's a good idea to create a 'quarantine' folder for all of your downloads, where they can be inspected before opening or unzipping.

Q&A Real world problems

A Result!

Q My son is spending a year in Mexico. We are e-mailing one another regularly and I would like to be able to send him the football results. He says that using the Internet to try to get the results is incredibly slow. Being a relative newcomer to the net I have been unable to save the football results as a file to attach to an e-mail. Would you please advise me of the most efficient way to do this?
D. B. via e-mail

A Most football results services on the Internet use fairly elaborate tables that can take a long time to send and may not survive intact when sent as attachments. However, several sites present the figures as plain text, that can be sent as an e-mail. Mabel's Tables (http://members.aol.com /mabstabs/daily.html) works well. Simply highlight the results table and copy it into the Windows Clipboard using Ctrl + C. You can tidy it up by pasting it into an open word processor page, or paste it directly into an e-mail window.

There is also an e-mail service that delivers football results and updated league tables for the Premiership, Nationwide Divisions 1, 2 and 3 and the results for the Worthington Cup and the FA Cup. You can subscribe by going to http://www.graphite.demon.co.uk/ – just click on the Stat-Mail icon.

Malevolent mail

Q I am a volunteer with the Citizens' Advice Bureau. We have just got onto the Internet and started using e-mail as the initial step out of the dark ages. We have been warned of two viruses being passed round via e-mail. Both are said to wipe the hard disk. Can viruses be transmitted via e-mail? If they are new, can virus checkers detect them?
A. B. via e-mail

A An e-mail message cannot on its own contain a virus: e-mail is simply text and has no programming capabilities. However, viruses can be carried on the back of e-mail as attachments. In order to activate the virus the file has to be opened or executed. The actual risk of you being sent a virus is fairly small but to be on the safe side, never open an attachment unless you are expecting it, or have requested it and you know what it contains. Always run downloaded files through your virus checker first. While it is true that new viruses are being created all the time, and virus checkers may not have it in their 'library', viruses tend to have predictable behaviour patterns and 'signatures', that checkers can spot. Most anti-viral programs can be regularly updated via the Internet.

Wipe the slate

Q   Lately I have noticed my copy of Windows is dumping a few too many .tmp files in the Temporary folder, moreover Temporary Internet has suddenly gained a few cache folders holding some very odd files. I have reformatted my hard drive once before but that was with the help of the manufacturer's help line. Unfortunately I can't remember how I did it so I would like to know if there are any books that include an idiot's guide to hard drive re-formatting, preferably in simple steps.
M. T. Northampton

A   Reformatting your hard drive should be an absolute last resort. It's not unheard of for manufacturer's technical help lines tend to suggest this remedy when faced with problems they either can't resolve or be bothered to sort out. A few temporary files hardly seem like a good enough reason to carry out such as drastic and time-consuming procedure. One reason why temporary files get left behind is that the application that created them isn't shut down properly; always check the System Tray on the Task Bar to make sure no programs are left running before you exit Windows. The extra folders generated by Temporary Internet are quite harmless and the files inside can be safely removed, though you may want to hang on to any 'cookies' for sites that you visit regularly as they can help speed up downloads. You can delete any files ending with .tmp using Windows Explorer, though bear in mind what we said earlier and don't empty the Recycle Bin straight away.

Better still, use a Windows housekeeping program, such as Clean-Sweep, to search out and eliminate unwanted files.

Free lunch...

Q First impressions of the Dixons Freeserve free Internet service are very favourable. However, a side-effect is that installing the software has resulted in the 'FS' logo appearing as a watermark across the button bar of Windows Explorer. How can I remove this unwanted graffiti?
D. B. via e-mail

A You must know there's no such thing as a free lunch and that graffiti, as you call it, is one of the prices you have to pay for this sort of service. However, it is easy enough to remove the Freeserve artwork and icons. They're contained in the Internet Explorer directory in a file called Signup. The toolbar is called toolbar.bmp, and the icons on the top right of the screen are: 22.bmp, 22S.bmp, 2238.bmp and 38S.bmp. It's a good idea to rename or copy them to another file, rather than simply delete them, just in case. After you've done that you will have to re-boot Windows, and Explorer should return to its default layout.

There is also an Internet site with full instructions on how to get rid of Freeserve from your desktop: http://members.xoom.com/Instigator/freeserve.

It's also worth reading through the very informative FAQ (frequently asked questions) on the Freeserve web site: http://www.freeserve.net/support.

Scan plan

Q I have a friend whose son is travelling the world and I am sending and receiving e-mail for them. The question I would like to ask, if I am given a typed letter is there a way I could scan it and send it using CompuServe?
J. P. via e-mail

A There are two possibilities. If your scanner came with OCR (optical character recognition) software, convert the letter into a plain text file and send that as a normal e-mail. Alternatively, scan the letter, save it as a JPEG file and send it as an e-mail attachment using the 'Attach File' button on the Create File window (or 'Send File', on the Mail drop-down menu).

E-Mall spolling

Q   My pelling is trrific but my typing is less so and I would dearly love to spllcheck this message before sending oit to you. However, Outlook Express Help tells me that it only supports spellcheck if I have MS Word, Excel or PowerPoint. As a Lotus fan I don't. Is there any way in which this can be fixed? I don't want to get into MS politics but this does seem a misuse of a quasi monopoly.
P. R. via e-mail

A   There are several spellcheckers that will work within Outlook (and a good many other e-mail programs). They are AutoSpell and Speller, both of which are available as try-before-you-buy shareware on the Internet. A brief description and links to file downloads can be found at http://www.spellchecker.com/mscscfi/overview.html.

Compu-save

Q   I have given up my CompuServe account and moved to Freeserve. I am also changing computers. How can I save all the hundreds of documents stored in the CompuServe Filing Cabinet somewhere else, without having to open each message individually and then save it? Is there any way of getting into Filing Cabinet?
J. W. via e-mail

A   The contents of the CompuServe Filing Cabinet is readable as plain text. Use Windows Explorer to open your CompuServe folder (it might be stored under Program Files), look for a sub-folder called FCabinet, open that and double-click on Fcabinet.dat. This will open WordPad and you'll be able to treat is as one long text file. Alternatively, find and open Fcabinet.dat with your preferred word processor.

Express answer

Q Can you please tell me how to copy a piece of mail that is in one of my Outlook Express folders into a Word document? When I try to use the 'Insert File' command in Word I am not able to identify an individual file in Outlook Express.
T. G. via e-mail

A Open and display the message in Outlook Express. Highlight the part you wish to use and press Ctrl + C (copy to Clipboard), open the Word document, put the cursor where you want the letter to appear and press Ctrl + V (paste command). Alternatively open the Outlook Express message window in a Word document, highlight, click, hold, drag and drop into Word.

CHAPTER 6   **Computer networks**

*On their own PCs are pretty impressive, but
connect them together and you'll see something
really amazing!*

A network is basically two or more PCs communicating with one another. It could be something as simple as a laptop or palmtop swapping files with a desktop machine, a group of PCs in an office sharing common resources such as files and directories or printers and modems, or the mother of all networks, the Internet. In an ideal world connecting computers together should be easy, as indeed it is if you own an Apple Mac, but the original IBM PC upon which all Windows machines are based was designed as a stand-alone device.

Getting PCs to communicate with one another can be horribly complicated, involving more technical gobbledegook and acronyms than you can shake a stick at. Thankfully Windows 95 and 98 have taken much of the sting out of getting hooked up to the Internet, but simple one-to-one connections can still cause major headaches. We'll begin by looking at how networks operate. Later on we'll show how to set up Windows 95/98 built-in networking facilities for a PC to PC connection, known as the Direct Cable Connection or DCC to its friends (and many enemies).

Computer networks take many different forms but the commonest type is the local area network or LAN, where all of the computers are physically close to one another in the same room, office or building. LANs can be further sub-divided into two types. Larger networks use what is known as a 'client/server' system with a fast and powerful central computer, called the server, running a network operating system (NOS) program that controls and communicates with all of the client PCs. The second type of LAN, and the one most appropriate for home and small office use, is the 'Peer to Peer' network, where all of the PCs have a common status and share and have access to each other's resources (disk drives, printers etc.).

Networked computers communicate using a common language or 'Network Protocol'. The two most widely used protocols are Ethernet (mostly used on LAN systems) and TCP/IP (transmission control protocol/Internet protocol) which is the language of the Internet. The Ethernet protocol works by sending data in small bursts or 'packets' along the cable connecting the PCs. Each PC in the network has to be fitted with a Network Interface Card or NIC that has a unique identity code or address, so it receives only data specifically meant for it. An Ethernet network can only handle one packet of data at a time but since data travels down the wires at the speed of light, and many millions of packets can be sent every second, it appears to operate more or less instantaneously.

The last consideration is how all of the computers are wired up, otherwise known as the network topology. There are three basic options, known as Bus, Ring or Star: most Ethernet LANs use bus or star topologies, so we'll look at those in more detail. In a bus system each PC in the network plugs into a wall socket or is jointed to a cable that runs

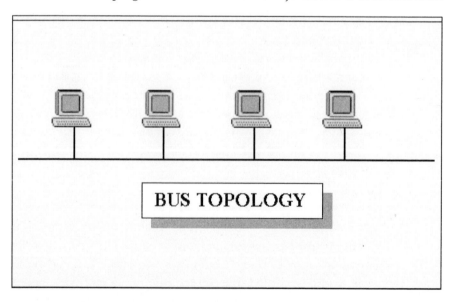

An example of bus topology, where all of the PCs in a network connect to a single cable running around the office or building

around the office or building. In a star system each PC is individually connected to a device called a distribution hub. It's a bit like a telephone exchange that routes the data, administers the system and looks after all of the network's resources. Bus systems are easy to install but are more prone to cabling faults and errors that can bring down the whole network. Star networks are more complicated and require additional hardware, but they are much more robust and tolerant of faults.

That's all very interesting but if all you want to do is exchange a few large files between your laptop and office PC, or use an old redundant PC as a backup machine, it's unlikely you'll be interested in getting involved with serious network paraphernalia. Other than physically moving data from one PC to another on floppy disks or removable storage media (Zip, Jazz, CD-R/RW disks etc.) or sending files to your other PC over the Internet, your home network options are dictated by the communications facilities on your PCs.

Broadly speaking there are two possibilities: you can connect the PCs together using serial/parallel cables or exchange data by cordless infrared or wireless links. A growing number of laptops and palmtop PCs have infrared data transfer facilities that operate without wires over a distance of a few metres. Unfortunately few desk-top machines

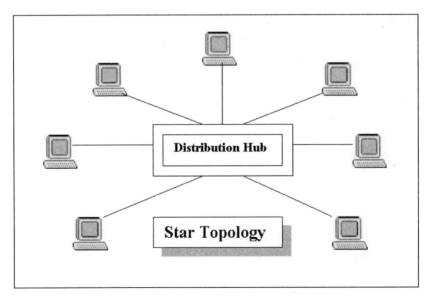

Star topology, where all of the PCs in a network connect to a central 'hub'

have it fitted as standard but it is possible to get hold of plug-in adaptors and communications software (infrared utilities are also included with the latest versions of Windows). Wireless links are also dependent on extra hardware to send and receive data via a pair of radio transmitters and receivers (transceivers) connected to both machines; however, the technology is in its infancy and there are still a lot of problems to be resolved.

That leaves a direct cable connection between the two machines, which is far and away the best solution for most users since it is cheap and reliable. Nowadays virtually all handheld PCs and a few laptops come with docking stations or communications facilities for exchanging files with Windows desk-top PCs. You can also buy specialist data exchange programs such as LapLink, which work very well indeed but can be quite expensive. Alternatively you can use Windows Direct Cable Connection (DCC); the only problem with that is it can be difficult to set up. Data exchange on the PC involves many separate layers and operations so the two computers must be precisely configured. In short, there are plenty of things that can go wrong but with patience it can be made to work.

Projects

CREATING A HOME NETWORK

Networking two PCs using the Windows 95/98 DCC utility is actually quite simple, once you know how. DCC allows you to exchange files and share resources such as disk drives and printers. The only trouble is, Microsoft has made it difficult to set up by not providing adequate instructions, and to make matters worse Help is no help whatsoever.

Rather than get bogged down in lengthy explanations and what all the multitude of acronyms mean, we'll dive straight in with a simple step-by-step procedure that should get DCC up and running on two PCs in around 10 to 15 minutes.

Begin by getting hold of the right cable. There are two options: 'serial null modem' and 'parallel interlink/laplink', sometimes sold as a 'DCC cable'. Nothing else will work. A parallel cable connection is strongly recommended since data transfers are three or four times faster than a serial connection. The parallel cable connects to the PC's printer ports, sometimes labelled LPT1. If you want the two PCs to share a printer or parallel port scanner you will have to install a second parallel port. This is actually quite easy and you can find out how in Chapter 10.

Step two is to make sure the DCC is installed on both PCs. On Windows 95 you'll find it by clicking on Start > Programs > Accessories. In Windows 98 it should be in the Communications sub-folder on Accessories. If not, you need to install it from your Windows CD-ROM using Add/Remove Programs in Control Panel; you'll find DCC listed under Communications on the Windows Set-up tab.

Step three is to configure the two computers. Both PCs must have three items of software installed: A network protocol called IPX/SPX (a common language networked PCs use to communicate; others are available but for the sake of simplicity stick with this one first) plus two networking utilities, called Client For Microsoft Networks and File & Printer Sharing for Microsoft Networks. You may already have one or more of them on your systems: to find out click on to the Network icon in Control Panel and check the list on the Configuration tab. If you don't see IPX/SPX on the list click Add to display the Select Network Type box. Select Protocol and click Add > Microsoft > IPX/SPX Compatible Networks then OK and follow the instructions (you may be asked to insert your Windows CD-ROM and go through a restart). Don't forget to repeat this and the following steps on both machines.

A similar procedure is used to load Client For Microsoft Networks and File & Printer Sharing for Microsoft Networks. They are both installed from Network in Control Panel; Client For Microsoft Networks can be found by clicking Add > Client > Microsoft. For File & Printer Sharing go to Add > Service > Microsoft. When all three components have been loaded on both machines return to Network, highlight IPX/SPX Compatible Networks, click the Properties button then the Bindings tab. You should see Client For Microsoft Networks and File & Printer Sharing for Microsoft Networks listed, and both items should be checked. To round off this stage on each machine click OK to return to Network and select the Identification tabs. You now have to give each PC a unique name: it must not be more than 15 characters long or

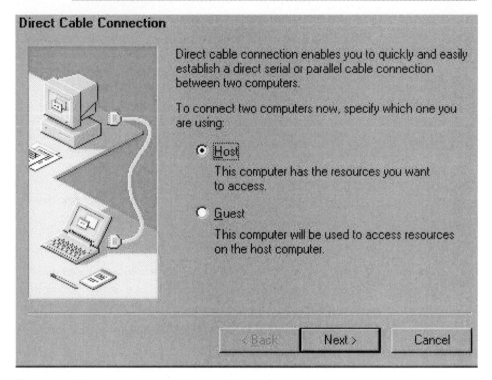

Direct Cable Connection

Direct cable connection enables you to quickly and easily establish a direct serial or parallel cable connection between two computers.

To connect two computers now, specify which one you are using:

◉ Host
This computer has the resources you want to access.

○ Guest
This computer will be used to access resources on the host computer.

| < Back | Next > | Cancel |

The Direct Cable Connection Wizard takes you through the setting up procedure

contain any space or non-alphanumeric characters. Keep them short and simple because you will need to key names in later on.

Now it's time to make the connection. Switch off both PCs and plug in the cable, re-boot and start with the PC that contains the files or resources you want to access (usually your desk-top PC). This machine will be called the 'Host', it's a bit like the server in a LAN. Next open Windows Explorer and decide which items you want to share with the other PC, right click on the file folder (or drive icon) and select Sharing, then the Sharing Tab and check 'Shared As'. If you want to move files in both directions you might want to enable sharing on the second PC or 'Guest' machine (your laptop or the computer you want to use to access files on the host).

The final step is to activate the DCC Wizard, which will start when you click on the Direct Cable Connection icon in Start > Programs > Accessories. Begin with the Host machine and follow the instructions:

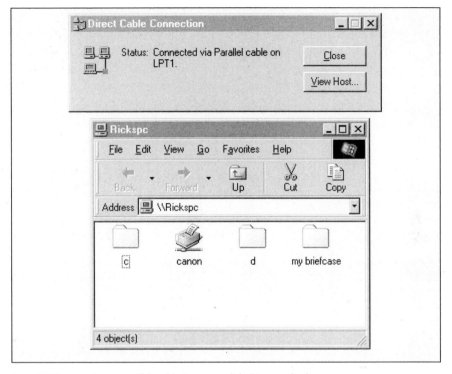

Once DCC is running you will be able to access disk drives and other
resources on the Host PC

you will be asked to select Host or Guest, which sort of cable you are
using and port (parallel and LPT1 if you've taken our advice). It's a
good idea to leave passwords fields blank at this stage (you can fiddle
around with those the next time you start DCC), click OK and Finish;
the host PC will now go into a waiting mode. Next run the DCC
Wizard on the Guest PC and make sure it is set up in exactly the same
way (parallel cable, LPT1 etc.). When you click on Finish the DCC
status window will change to show the two machines are talking to
each other. You will be asked to enter the name of the host PC and a
moment or two later a folder window should open, showing all of the
resources on the other machine that you can access; simply treat it as
another disk drive connected to your PC.

Hopefully it will go smoothly but if you encounter a problem here
are some things to check. Make sure you are using the right cable: ordinary parallel and serial cables are simply no good. The parallel port

settings for both computers must be the same. The three common options are Normal EPP and ECP; you can change port settings in the PC's BIOS program (refer to the instruction manual or a PC savvy friend). The Network configuration for both machines must also be exactly the same. DCC sometimes seems to go to sleep and won't wake up so if you can't establish a link re-boot both PCs and run the DCC Wizards again. DCC may fail if the Network Neighbourhood icon has been removed from your desktop using Tweak UI. DCC doesn't get on well with other types of network: if your PC has been used on a network remove any old or unused protocols from Network in Control Panel.

Q&A **Real world problems**

Out cast

Q   My query concerns a box that appears when I start Internet Explorer 4 (Freeserve) or Outlook Express. Following the usual splash screens but before the 'connect' box appears I am getting a small screen with the message 'WNetGetUser returned' this is followed by a line of symbols and characters (gibberish and always different) and then a button with 'OK'. Pressing OK clears the box and then the connection box appears. How do I stop it appearing?
B.S. via e-mail

A   This annoying behaviour is usually caused by the PC not having a valid 'name'. To properly christen your machine go to the Start menu then Settings > Control Panel > Network and click the Identification tab. Clear the name field and put in a name like 'default', if you decide to call it something else do not use any non-alphanumeric characters or spaces. If you don't see an Identification tab this is usually due to the fact that your machine has no Network Client installed. Open the Network icon in Control Panel and click on Add then double-click Client. In the manufacturer's box select Microsoft (assuming your PC is not connected to another network) and in the Network window opposite click on Client for Microsoft Networks then OK. You may be prompted to load your Windows 95 disk, follow the instructions and restart the PC. Go back to Network in Control Panel and the Identification tab should appear. Check that the name field is occupied (default or your name, but no non-alphanumeric characters or spaces) and re-try IE4 and Outlook. Hopefully the error message will no longer appear. You may find that you get a new Network Password dialogue box appearing - you can get rid of this from Network in Control Panel by highlighting 'Windows Logon' under Primary Network Logon field, click OK and re-start your PC.

Irritating icon

Q   A new icon has appeared on my desktop, namely 'Network Neighbourhood' and I also have a logon password box appearing and

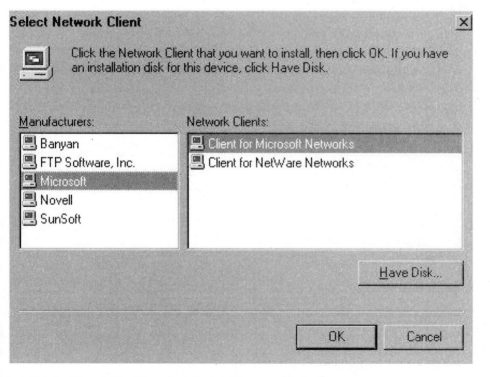

Installing the Network Client is a critical step in setting up a direct cable connection

'Log off John Smith' on the Start menu, which I do not recall seeing there before.

J. S. via e-mail

A   To remove the logon password boxes go to Find on the Start menu, in the 'Named' field type *.pwl and click Find Now. This will locate all instances of passwords on your PC. Rename the files with the suffix '.old' and restart the PC. If the password boxes reappear enter your username but leave the password field empty and press Enter. Restart and you shouldn't see them again.

The Network Neighbourhood icon and Log Off ... are both harmless and can be left alone. If you must, you can remove Network Neighbourhood with the Windows utility Tweak Ui.

Deleting the 'Log Off' entry is fairly straightforward but it involves editing the Registry file (definitely off limits to Windows novices). Do not try this unless you know exactly what you are doing, and always back up the Registry first – you have been warned!

Open Regedit and find the key: HKEY_CURRENT_USER\Software \Microsoft\Windows\CurrentVersion\Policies\Explorer. Create a new Binary Value (New on the Edit menu) and call it 'NoLogOff', right click on NoLogOff, select Modify and give it a value 01 00 00 00, close Regedit and restart the machine.

Wake up call

Q   I am running Windows 98 and have an external message modem. As messages and faxes are stored in the modem, this allows me to have a single telephone line and one device to act as a modem, answering machine and fax receiver without leaving my computer running. Unfortunately, Windows 98 switches the computer on every time the phone rings and I don't want, nor need this to happen. I come home from work to find the computer has been on all day, because someone's left a message on the answering machine! I have tried changing the power management settings and disabling power management altogether, but can't find a solution. Is there anything I can do, other than disconnecting the modem from the computer?

M. R. via e-mail

A   Many PCs have a 'wake up on modem ring' function in the power management section of the BIOS (basic input output system) program. To access the BIOS look for a message like 'press DEL on start-up' (or a combination of keys), while the computer is booting up.

Losing wait

Q   I have only one telephone line. If a caller rings me while I am on the Internet my phone rings and my net connection is broken off. Is there a way of preventing this?
M. F. via e-mail

A   You can temporarily disable Call Waiting by keying in # 43 # on your phone before you go on line, and switch it back on again afterwards using * 43 #.

Tapi zapper

Q   I am currently using CompuServe and when I exit the program a message always appears: 'The following applications are using the currently active dial-up networking connection - "Tapisrv.exe"'. Can you throw any light on this and advise how to stop it recurring?
J. J. via e-mail

A   This is a known problem with CompuServe version 3.0 and Windows 98. It can be cured with a downloadable patch. Click on Go, type File Downloads, double click File Finder choose All Files, enter Win98fix. exe in the Search field and follow the instructions.

Modem go slow?

Q   I have a 56 kbps modem, and the ISP I use states that it also uses 56 kbps modems, but I have never connected at more than 33.6 kbps. Is there any way that I can change this?
M. W. via e-mail

A   Many factors determine data transfer speeds, not least the time of day –
it falls off dramatically when Internet traffic increases during the after-
noon and early evening – and the quality of your telephone line. In any
event the maximum speed that you can upload data on a normal phone
line is 33.6 kbps, 56 kbps is only possible when downloading data, and
then only a 'perfect' line. You could ask BT to check your connection
and there are various tweaks they can make at their end to improve line
quality, but it's unlikely you will gain much. The only way to get a significant increase in speed is to upgrade to a digital (ISDN) line.

Split decision

Q   Early last year I took advantage of a BT offer to install a second line at
half the normal price, specifically for linking to the Internet. I hap-
pened to be at home when the BT engineers called and was amazed
that the entire process took only 20 minutes. The major part of the job
seemed to be the fitting of large plastic box adjacent to the main BT
junction box. This, they told me, was something to do with 'DACS'
which is a system for converting a single line into two lines. It seems to
have worked and I have had very few problems connecting to the Internet through my 28800 modem. I have recently seen on a newsgroup
I subscribe to, that, if using a 'DACS' line, you cannot use a modem faster
than 28800 kps. Does this mean it is pointless upgrading my modem?
C. C. via e-mail

A   The DACS or digital access carrier system splits a single line into two;
a DACS is normally only fitted when there is insufficient capacity for a
second line. BT say that it shouldn't have any effect on modems up to
33.3 kbps but add that BT salespeople are supposed to ask the cus-
tomer what they intend to use the line for. If it is for fast Internet access
they should be advised to consider the Highway or ISDN digital
options. BT advises that if you are having problems with faster modems ask BT to check the installation. We would be interested to hear
from any readers who have had direct experience – good or bad – with
a split line.

CHAPTER 7 **Using the Internet**

The Internet is an invaluable resource for finding people, from friends and relatives, to your early ancestors. It's all there, at the click of a mouse.

You know how it is, you meant to write or phone but ... It's all too easy to lose touch with family and friends over the years but when you want to track someone down who may not even live in this country anymore, where on earth do you start? Your PC, of course!

The Internet is jam-packed full of resources, directories and databases that can help you to find people, even if they are not Internet users themselves. Even so, with the number of people now connected and on-line there is a good chance that your search will quickly yield an e-mail address or phone number if not for the actual person, then a close relative who may be able to help.

Before you begin arm yourself with as many details as possible about the person you are trying to find. That includes obvious things like their full name, but it may also help to know apparently trivial facts, such as the name of the school, college or university they attended. Their occupation or membership of professional bodies or associations can often provide useful leads, as can any information about hobbies, interests and sporting activities.

Yahoo People Search, one of the most efficient e-mail search engines
on the net

Projects

FINDING PEOPLE ON THE NET

It is worth trying a basic e-mail search first; however, bear in mind that
there is no such thing as a central directory, nor is there likely to be for
quite some time. The Internet is simply too big and it is growing at a
phenomenal rate with new Internet Service Providers and 'domains'
coming on stream almost daily. Moreover, there is a significant churn
rate – especially in the UK – as users chop and change their ISPs, often
creating e-mail addresses that subsequently lapse into disuse.

Nevertheless, if the individual uses one of the longer established

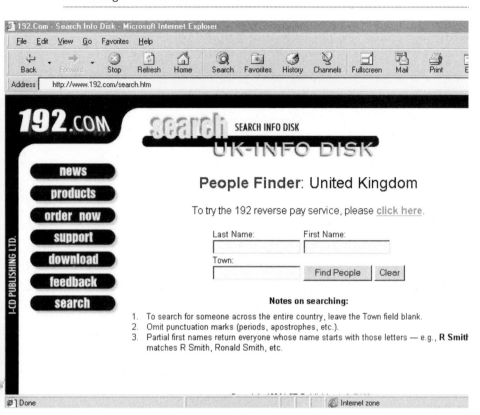

Looking for someone in the UK? Try a telephone search first

service providers your chances of success are quite good. The Yahoo People Search web site (http://people.yahoo.com/) is one of the best places to start. All you need is the person's surname and first name (always try both forename and initials); don't be surprised if you get multiple entries and a lot of irrelevant 'hits' from people with the same name, especially if it happens to be a common one. Even if you think the person is unlikely to have an e-mail address try it anyway, but if that doesn't work the next step is a telephone search.

There are several searchable residential and business telephone number databases, created from information available in the public domain (electoral register, commercial lists etc.). The UK Info Disk web site contains the telephone numbers of more than 42 million UK residents (www.192.com). It will search out an address and telephone number using just a surname, though refining the search with a first name or initials usually produces more manageable results. This site also gives you the opportunity to send a card, gift or flowers to the person. It is also possible to carry out a 'reverse' search if you are willing to buy a CD-ROM or pay a subscription. BT's phone directory has recently gone on-line at: http://www.bt.com/phonenetuk/ and there are also several commercial and business directories such as Thomson's (http://www.infospace.com/uk.thomw/) and Yellow Pages (http://www.yell.co.uk/) that may well help if you know the person's trade, business or profession.

Incidentally, if you are concerned about your own address and telephone number being available on the UK Info Disk or web site you can request that your entry be deleted.

If you are seeking someone who has moved abroad, and you know which country they are living in then there is a chance they'll be listed in one of the hundreds of searchable international telephone directories on the Internet. The Excite World People Finder web site has a list of almost 70 countries with links to residential and commercial directories (http://www.whowhere.lycos.com/wwphone/excite_world.html). The quality and depth of these directories varies from country to country but in many cases these are the country's main telecom company databases.

If phone and e-mail listings draw a blank, try using the person's name as a key word in any of the larger 'search engines', such as Alta-Vista, Infoseek, Lycos, WebCrawler, Yahoo etc. You may well come across a family 'home page', possibly with links to the individual or his or her relatives.

If you are attempting to trace old school or college friends then use a search engine to find out whether the school or university has its own web site. Many of them have alumni notice boards dedicated to finding old boys and old girls, often with details of recent or forthcoming class reunions. You may even be able to post a 'wanted' notice in the hope that ex pupils and students may still be in contact with the person you are seeking.

Although few clubs and associations post details of members on their web pages it is well worth e-mailing or writing to membership secretaries of relevant organisations, asking if the person you are looking for is known to them and, if so, to pass on your message.

USING YOUR PC FOR RESEARCH

It might be stretching the point a wee bit to suggest that computers are the fount of all knowledge but the fact is, if you have a question – no matter how complex or trivial it might be – your PC can almost certainly help you to find the answer. Note the use of the word 'help': computers are merely tools, albeit extremely versatile ones with a huge capacity for storing and retrieving information, but that's all they are, and like any tool, it works best when you know how to use it properly.

Essentially there are three ways your PC can assist with research. You can look for information on a 'local' database, such as a CD-ROM. If you have an Internet connection you have access to a worldwide network of databases and sources of information, and you can use e-mail and Newsgroups to communicate directly with people and organisations.

Information on CD-ROM is mostly in the form of broad-based ency-clopaedias or specialist or single-subject titles. Multimedia encyclopae-dias are the best source for what might be called general-purpose infor-mation, that is basic facts and figures about people and places, history the arts and science. Specialist CD-ROMs are a bit of a mixed bag – there are some very good ones around and lots of really amateurish ones, some are worse than useless, so tread carefully.

CD-ROMs have two big plus points, they are quick – no waiting for a connection and no data bottlenecks during peak times – plus they are normally easy to use. You won't have to sift through stacks of irrele-vant information and no extra additional costs will be incurred if you wander off the topic or get side-tracked. Most CD-ROM encyclopae-dias will allow you to cut and paste text and pictures from the disk into a word processor document, though you should be aware that mater-ial is usually subject to copyright and not for publication.

At the last count there were more than a dozen CD-ROM ency-clopaedias on the market but two stand head and shoulders above the rest. They are *Microsoft Encarta*, and *Encyclopaedia Britannica*. Encarta is the world's most popular CD-ROM encyclopaedia, it is well presented and it covers a lot of ground. The latest 'Reference Suite' is a well-researched 'British' edition and includes a world atlas and Bookshelf (dictionary, thesaurus etc.). DVD versions of Encarta and Britannica are now available.

Encyclopaedia Britannica on CD-ROM is the disk version of the world's most respected reference work. The multimedia content (pictures, sound movies etc.) is still some way behind Encarta but what it lacks in glitz it more than makes up for with solid, authoritative content. The cost of Britannica has fallen dramatically in the past two years and the most recent edition sells for less than one tenth of the cost of the hardback version!

If you're on a tight budget there are several perfectly adequate CD-ROM Encyclopaedias such as Compton's and Hutchinson (http://www.bt-ern.co.uk/helicon) costing less than £30. Moreover, it's worth keeping an eye out for freebies on PC magazines though they may be an older version of a new current offering.

SEARCHING THE INTERNET

If the information you're after is of a more specific nature and not the sort of thing that's likely to be found on CD-ROM, you'll probably find it on the Internet, but only if you know where to look. The trouble with the Internet is that it is so big that it can make finding a needle in a haystack look simple. Unless you have the address or URL of a particular web site you know has the information you're seeking you will have to call upon the services of a search engine. They are the telephone directories, Yellow Pages and guide books to the Internet rolled into one, with a dash of advertising thrown in for good measure. The good news is that most of them are completely free to use.

There are many to choose from, the best known being AltaVista, Lycos, HotBot, Infoseek and Yahoo. To access any of them simply open your browser and in the address field type www. then the name of the search engine and add the suffix .com, e.g. :

- www.yahoo.com.
- www.altavista.com
- www.infoseek.com
- www.lycos.com
- www.webcrawler.com

Search engines use keywords to find web pages containing the information you want and this is where things can go awry. The trick is to narrow your search by choosing your words very carefully. Search engines work in slightly different ways so it pays to get to know their little foibles. Most will carry out a search using just two or three words,

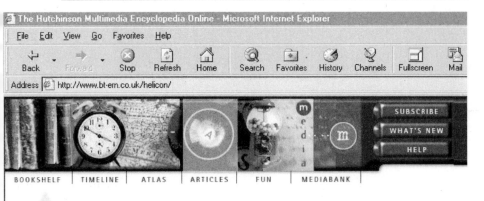

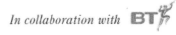

On-line encyclopaedias can be a very good source of information

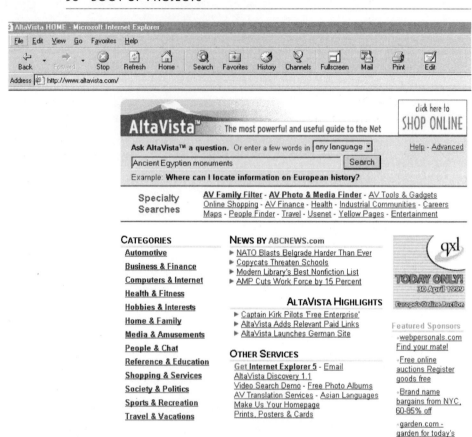

Begin researching a subject by using one of the main search engines

others, like AltaVista, can understand simple phrases, such as 'where can I find …' or 'what is the population of …'. The main search engines are usually the best place to start; most of them will obligingly point you towards more specialist search sites covering narrower fields of interest.

Incidentally, several of the CD-ROM encyclopaedias have their own web sites: most search engines include links to them, Britannica On-Line is also worth a visit and although this is a subscription service you can try a free sample search at www.eb.com.

The text and pictures appearing on web sites can usually be copied and pasted into word processor documents. However, if the words on a web page won't highlight when you click and drag the mouse pointer then it is probably an image, rather than text. In that case you won't be able to extract the words and numbers, though you can still save the image to the Windows clipboard by pressing the Prtscn (print screen) key on the keyboard and viewing the image using PaintBox or your chosen graphics program. Once again be careful that you do not infringe anyone's copyright if you are going to use the material in a publication or book.

CREATING A FAMILY TREE

Your PC's ability to gather, store and process information makes it a perfect tool for genealogical research, and this is a good excuse to make a start on that family tree you've been meaning to compile. It can be an absorbing and rewarding pastime and who knows where it might lead? You might discover royal ancestry, a hereditary title and coat of arms, a forgotten legacy or even an infamous mass murderer in the family. The point is you'll be creating a unique and valuable resource to share with the whole family and a fascinating insight into your own life and times for future generations.

A computer makes the task so much easier by creating a dynamic database and archive that can easily be updated as family members arrive and depart, but the real advantage lies in the ways different types of information can be collated and presented. The traditional hand-drawn family tree usually has room only for names and key dates; a PC family tree can incorporate so much more, including almost unlimited amounts of background notes, stories or anecdotes, photographs, drawings, scans of old newspapers, even sound and video clips. The PC has another equally important role to play, as a finder of information. The Internet is brim-full of genealogical sites, family home pages and e-mail provides a fast and efficient means of communication for family members, wherever they may be.

So where do you start? You will of course need a PC but this kind of application isn't particularly demanding and any reasonably recent multimedia model (Pentium 90 or faster) will suffice. An Internet connection is vital and since you will be handling photographs and documents, a scanner is invaluable. Again, you won't need a particularly elaborate model, indeed any of the current budget models should be more than adequate.

The right software is important too. It is possible to create a basic graphical tree with standard Windows applications like a word processor. Better still would be a spreadsheet program, such as Excel. Cells can contain a mixture of information and the tabular presentation is well suited to the tree layout.

However, to do the job properly and make maximum use of your PC's processing power it's a good idea to get hold of a purpose-designed family tree program. There are plenty to choose from, including some excellent freeware and shareware titles that can be downloaded from the Internet (http://www.hotfiles.com/home/genealogy.html). Programs to look out for include Broderbund Family Tree Maker, GSP Family Tree, Cumberland Family Tree, Family Origins and Generations, most of which sell for between £20 and £40.

In addition to displaying the tree in a visually attractive format, and making it easier to access or update the archive, most family tree programs will allow you to create detailed printouts or even help compile an illustrated book for wider distribution. Many family tree programs use a common file format, called Gedcom (extension *.gft), which will allow you to exchange data with other researchers, using other types of software.

It can be a lot of hard work so before you begin ask around to see if any of the initial research has already been done. Most families have at least one amateur historian – past or present – whose records may be able to get you off to a good start. Older family members can give you first-person access to recent family history, though remember to exercise some tact and always be sensitive to any skeletons and scandals that you may uncover. Illegitimacy and extra marital affairs were just as common 100 years ago as they are today, our forebears were just more adept at keeping them secret.

Official documents such as old birth, marriage and death certificates are an invaluable source of raw data and family photo albums can provide a wealth of information. Don't dismiss the apparently mundane: postcards and letters often contain useful historical snippets and even obscure photographs of places or buildings can provide additional avenues for exploration.

Back to the PC. Start with an Internet search of your family name on

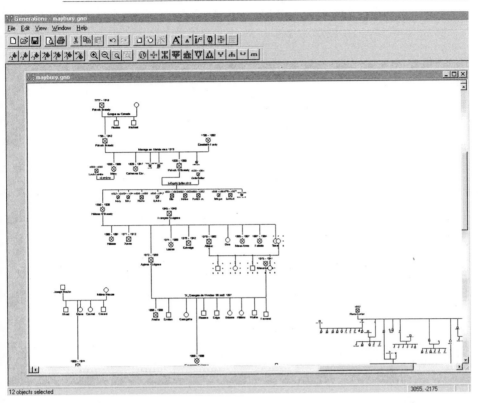

An example of a family tree from Generations, a simple to use freeware program downloaded from the Internet

search engines such as Alta Vista, Yahoo and Lycos; don't forget to try some of the more obvious alternative spellings. You may well come across a family home page, a link to long-lost relations or overseas branches of the family.

In the UK genealogists are well served by our long history of bureaucracy and record keeping by government agencies. The Public Records Office web site (http://www.pro.gov.uk) has some excellent information and advice for novice family historians. Try also the Office for National Statistics and Family Record Centre (http://www.ons.gov.uk/ons_f.htm) and the Commonwealth War Graves Commission (http://www.cwgc.org/cwgchome.htm), all of whom host informative web sites.

You will also come across numerous historical societies, research

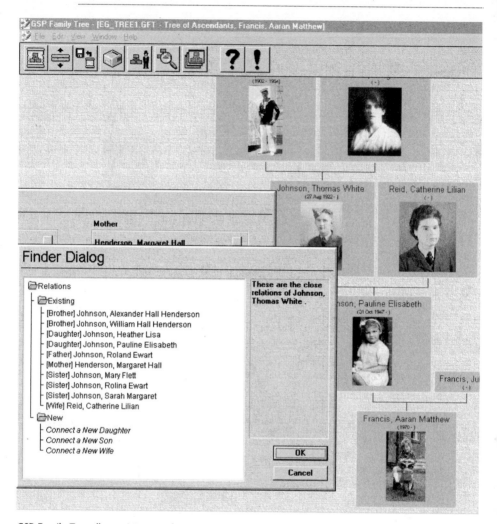

GSP Family Tree allows pictures to be incorporated into the finished document

agencies and magazines that specialise in genealogical research. An excellent site to start off with is Family Chronical (http://www.familychronical.com). The world's largest genealogical database has been set up by the Church of the Latter-Day Saints in the US (http://www.familysearch.org/). It is extremely powerful - avoid a casual search, you will be swamped with information but it should prove invaluable once you have started work on your family tree.

Be realistic in your research and set yourself achievable goals. At first it is highly unlikely you will be able to trace your ancestry back more than a few generations, so aim to complete a tree for the past 200 years and take it from there. Most researchers begin with the paternal or family name but from a genetic perspective the maternal line is equally valid and in some societies it is considered more important, though it may involve considerably more effort.

ACCESSING NEWSGROUPS

Newsgroups are the heart and soul of the Internet. Think of them as the community halls of the global village, far removed from the slick big-city commercial and business interests on the world wide web. They're places where like-minded individuals meet on-line to discuss and swap ideas, ask and answer questions on just about any subject you care to name (and one or two you probably wouldn't).

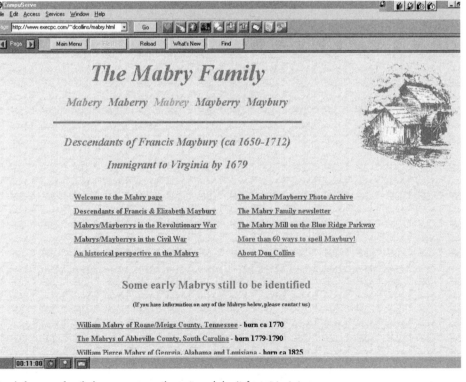

Look for your family home page on the net, and don't forget to try some alternative spellings

A newsgroup is a public noticeboard where you can post e-mail messages, articles or announcements for others to read and respond to. Unlike normal e-mail and the web, which are immediately accessible once you've signed up with an Internet Service Provider (ISP), you have to actively 'subscribe' to Newsgroups, though it's not like a magazine or newspaper subscription and it won't cost you a penny (apart from your normal on-line charges).

If you are wondering if there's a newsgroup devoted to your particular interests the answer is undoubtedly yes. It's impossible to give a precise figure but there are well over 40,000 of them right now, with hundreds more being created every day. The number of newsgroups you will have direct access to depends on your ISP. Newsgroups are stored on computers called news servers, which are part of a wider network called Usenet; apart from the problems of finite storage space most ISPs restrict or prohibit newsgroups devoted to activities they deem antisocial or undesirable (child pornography, bomb-making, software piracy, that kind of thing). Newsgroups may also be 'moderated', that is monitored for abusive or offensive messages, to keep respondents on the subject and prevent blatant advertising. In fact there is a fairly strict code of conduct or 'netiquette' that most newsgroup users are happy to adhere to.

In order to access newsgroups you will need a program called a newsreader. The chances are you already have one on your PC as they are integrated into most popular browsers and e-mail programs, including Internet Explorer, Netscape Navigator and those supplied by AOL and CompuServe. Separate newsreader software programs are also available, one of the most popular being a shareware program called Free Agent, which can be downloaded from http://www.forteinc.com.

The first job is to set up your newsreader. You will need a couple of items of information, namely your e-mail address and the domain name of your ISP's news server. You should find this included in the sign-up information or you can get it from the ISP's helpline – it will usually be something like 'news.freebienet.co.uk'. In Outlook Express set-up begins when you click the Read News icon on the opening page, just follow the instructions and when it has finished you will be asked if you want to download the list of Newsgroups on the ISP's news server. This can take several minutes depending on the speed of your

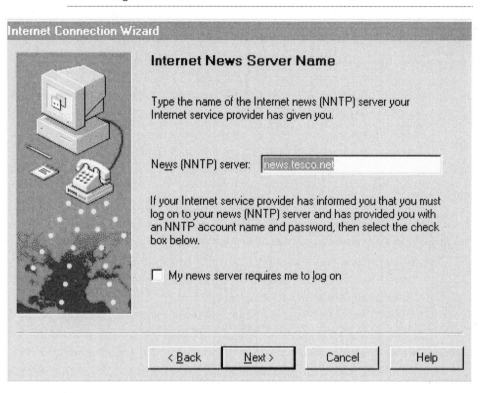

Use the Internet Newsgroup Setup Wizard to find the topics that
interest you

connection and time of day. You have to do this only once since most
newsreaders will automatically update the list when you are on-line.

The newsreader will log off and present you with a list of several
thousand newsgroups. Don't bother searching through them all, it will
take forever, your newsreader has a search facility that looks for groups
containing a keyword. You can then select the ones that interest you by
clicking on the subscribe button. Incidentally, you might be wondering
what all the prefixes mean. Any newsgroup beginning with comp.
means it is computer related, misc. is miscellaneous, rec. is short for
recreational subjects, sci. is used for science-related topics, soc. covers
social issues, and so on. By far the largest collection of newsgroups
begin with alt. for alternative. The alt. groups are a kind of fringe operation, existing outside of the official Usenet system but that doesn't
imply they're any less interesting, relevant or useful, though this tends
to be where the dubious and doubtful newsgroups congregate.

Once you have chosen the groups you wish to subscribe to you will have to go back on line (Connect icon on the Outlook Express toolbar). Now the newsreader will download all of the 'headers' in your selected groups. Headers are topics or subject headings (by default Outlook Express loads 300 headers – you can change it by going to Options on the Tools menu and selecting the Read tab). Depending on the newsgroup you may see anything from a dozen to several hundred postings, those marked with a plus sign indicate the message is part of a 'thread', effectively a running conversation with other newsgroup users contributing to the topic.

You can read any message simply by clicking on the header; however, all the time you are on-line you are clocking up the phone bill. The alternative is to download selected messages – or the whole newsgroup, if there's not too many of them – and read them at your leisure, off-line. In Outlook Express the option to mark and download messages can be found on the Tools menu.

You will probably find that some messages or articles no longer exist or you get an error message. Don't worry, it's not a fault on your PC – messages are routinely deleted, to make way for new ones and on really busy newsgroups postings may only be shown for a couple of days. After reading a few messages you might well decide that you have something to contribute or a question to ask, but it is a good idea to read all of the postings in your chosen group. It's worth monitoring a newly subscribed newsgroup for a while to get a feel of how it works, pick up the jargon and maybe get to know the people using it. Many newsgroups include a FAQ (frequently asked questions) file about the group and you should read it.

LEARNING NETIQUETTE

Having subscribed to a newsgroup most newcomers feel an irresistible urge to join in. Don't – at least, not straight away. You will almost certainly commit some terrible *faux pas* and irritate or enrage other members of the group who will respond with 'flames' or 'mail bombs', by sending you abusive and offensive e-mails. If you want to get the most out of this amazing resource you must learn a few simple rules; it is called 'netiquette' and you ignore it at your peril.

It might sound a bit precious, but remember there are people on the other side of your computer screen, thousands, possibly millions of them! It is very easy to offend when your only means of communication is a keyboard. Those reading your words may well come from very different cultural and ethnic backgrounds and English might not be their first language. Without voice inflections, facial expressions and the body language of face-to-face conversation a seemingly innocent remark or gentle British irony can turn into a major insult, which in other circumstances might result in a punch on the nose!

Good netiquette isn't meant to be stuffy, your messages should be informal but polite and above all succinct and to the point; long and wordy postings will simply be ignored. Sarcasm and humour should be used with caution, if you must try to be funny then make sure your wit is well signposted - we'll show you how to do that in a moment.

There are a few other points to bear in mind. DON'T SHOUT unless you really mean it, writing in uppercase is considered bad form. If you want to respond to a specific point or communicate directly with a member of the group on a topic outside the newsgroups subject area, send an e-mail to the member concerned otherwise a newsgroup can quickly become cluttered with irrelevant messages or 'follow-ups'. If you have a point to make, it is helpful to others if you summarise what has been said before but avoid needless repetition. If you cite references or quotes make sure you mention the source, do not infringe commercial copyright and be very careful about what you say about others. Don't forget newsgroups are in the public domain and your comments can easily be read or forwarded by e-mail to those you've maligned. Always, always check spelling and grammar but avoid criticising others' use of English: for all you know they might suffer from dyslexia or are learning the language.

It sounds like there's a lot to learn but it is mostly common sense and it is surprising how quickly you can pick it up by sitting on the sidelines for a couple of weeks and just reading the postings. You can get a crash course in netiquette by looking at the guidelines and FAQs in your own newsgroup and there are some useful hints and tips on the web at http://www.fau.edu/netiquette/net/elec.html, or try the newsgroup 'news.announce.newusers', which is aimed at newcomers.

Newsgroup postings are often littered with acronyms. Used wisely they are a useful form of shorthand but too many will make your mes-

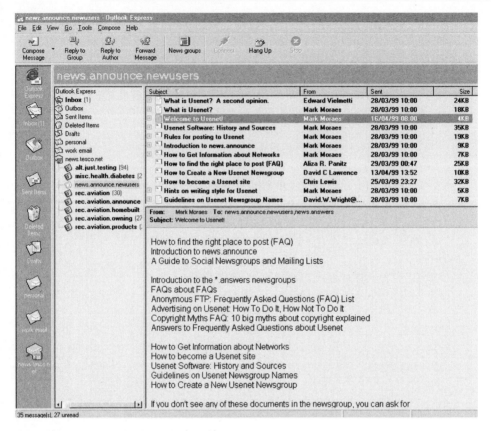

Internet Newsgroups, a great way to share ideas

sages unreadable or difficult to follow. It's worth committing half a dozen or so of the most commonly used ones to memory. They include FYI, which means 'for your information', BTW is 'by the way', IMHO stands for 'in my humble/honest opinion', ROTFL, 'rolling on the floor laughing', RTFM means 'read the flipping manual' (or words to that effect …), TIA is 'thanks in advance' and TTFN, 'ta-ta for now'; a more complete list can be found at http://www.fau.edu/netiquette /net/acroynms.txt

Since you will be using plain text to compose your messages it is useful to know how to emphasise words or phrases. Surrounding words with *asterisks* draws attention to it, rather like an underline or a bold typeface. Names and titles, like _Boot Up_ can be signified with a single underscore before and after and it is a good idea to limit line length to no more than 60 or 70 characters as this could make your messages difficult to read on some newsreaders.

A good way of writing between the lines, to let those reading your postings know you are making a joke or what you are thinking, is to use simple graphics made up of text characters. They are called 'emoticons' and there are dozens of them: for a complete listing look at http://www.eff.org/papers/eeftti/eeg_287.html.

The most basic emoticon is the 'smiley' made up of a colon, dash and close bracket symbol thus :-) (if you don't get it, turn the page on its side). There are some really ingenious ones, like ; -) which suggests the user has just made a sarcastic remark and is winking, or }:-(for the user is wearing a toupee on a windy day.

Finally a few more simple and mostly obvious 'don'ts'. Do not use newsgroups to advertise. There's no harm in mentioning useful or apposite products and services in response to a newsgroup posting, even if they are your own, but blatent advertising is frowned upon. It

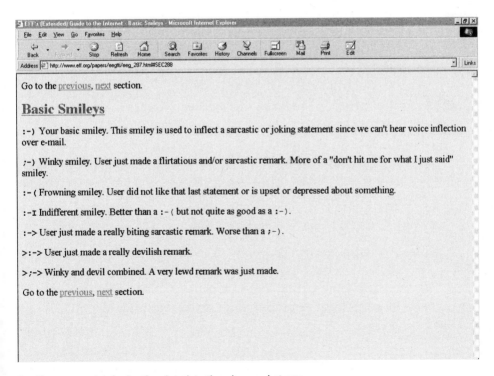

Emoticons are a simple shorthand, to let others know what you are thinking

is counter productive – you will be flamed, excluded from the group and you could end up with some very harmful things being written about you and your business. From time to time you may see or be sent chain letters promising all kinds of things or making worthy sounding appeals. Bin them all. They are invariably scams or mathematically impossible; moreover they waste valuable (and limited) network resources. If they are traced back to you, your Internet account will almost certainly be closed.

Once you've served your apprenticeship you will want to post your first message, do not send a 'This is a test' message to your group, unless you want your e-mail box filled with flames. There are newsgroups like alt.just.testing where you can check to make sure everything is working properly.

Q&A   **Real world problems**

Mute modem

Q   I have an annoying problem, that I cannot solve. With my previous computer whenever I logged on to my server I heard the modem chirrup away as it made contact. I now have a Tiny Pentium that remains obstinately silent, but only in this respect. At all other times the machine signals me in all the usual ways. Have I inadvertently switched something off?
G. B. via e-mail

A   There is control for modem sound in the Windows 95 Control Panel. Double-click on the Modems icon, select the General tab, highlight your modem's entry, click on the Properties button, select the General tab and you'll find the speaker slider control in the middle.

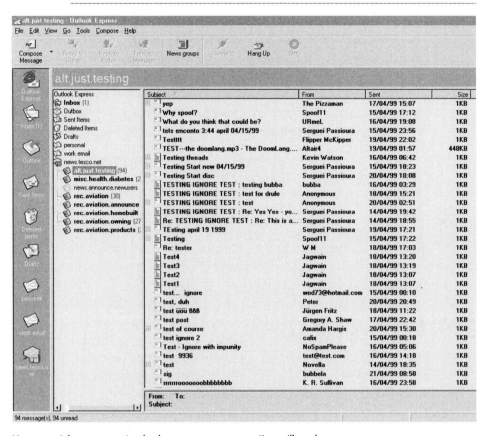

Use a special newsgroup to check your newsgroup posting will work

Zip zap?

Q   I have downloaded several programs from the Internet in the form of
.zip files which I place in a folder that I have allocated for this purpose,
called (predictably) 'Downloads'. Having unzipped the programs, they
then take up residence in their own specific folders as any other ordinary program would do. However, I notice that the original .zip file is
still in my 'Download' folder.

   Would I be correct in assuming that I may safely delete these .zip files
since they are now duplicates (albeit in a compressed form) of the programs that are now up and running on my computer?
J. L. via e-mail

A   Yes, you can remove the original downloaded .zip files, but it's a bit like throwing away a program's original installation disk. You might need it one day if, for example, a program is corrupted or you want to load it on another machine – there's no guarantee the program will always be available from the Internet. If you need to recover space on your hard disk drive then copy the original .zip file to a floppy disk or another suitable backup medium.

Ten minute rule ...

Q   As a parent of three highly PC literate children, I used to spend a great deal of time controlling and limiting their computer usage. Since installing a new home system I have overcome this problem – and seen the last of a lot of arguments – by the use of a reasonably cost-effective shareware package. This allows me to control the time an individual spends on the system, the hours of the day they can use it and several other useful bells and whistles.

However, the new PC has heralded the arrival of the Internet into the H household, which brings another set of problems. There is a plethora of software to control the content that they can view from the net, but as yet I have not found anything which controls the length of time a user spends on the Internet so that I can, for instance, limit them to perhaps 10 minutes each a day. Our ISP is Freeserve, which doesn't appear to give this functionality. Have you any suggestions?
J. H. via e-mail

A   Only ten minutes, that's a bit mean ... The answer to your question is yes; there are several web utilities that can be programmed to monitor the time spent on-line, sound an alarm when time has expired and even automatically disconnect the line, if required. Clockwise and WebNik are almost certainly what you are looking for and they can be downloaded from the excellent Tucows web site, along with details of more than a dozen other shareware web timers: http://tucows.cableinet.net/time95.html.

Phone connection

Q   I have heard that there is software that will allow me to call a standard telephone using my PC via the Internet, i.e. worldwide calls at local rates. I know several people who've heard of it but no one knows where I can buy or download the program. Any ideas?
D. L. via e-mail

A   The best-known Internet PC-to-phone utility is Net2Phone but it may not be quite as cheap as you imagine. Calls from your PC are routed through the Net2Phone web site and then on to local servers that make the connection to the telephone network in the country you are calling. In addition to normal on-line charges (the cost of a local call in your case) there is an additional subscription payment and variable call rate, depending on the country. You can get more details and download free-trial access software from: http://www.net2phone.com.

Family disk

Q   I have recently begun to research my family history using Family Tree Maker software on my ageing 486 DX PC. I am thinking of updating my PC. Before I consider the specification, is there any way of calculating the amount of disk space required for, say, a scanned 7 × 5-inch family group photograph, and thence the space needed for a bag full of pictures that I have, covering the last 100 years?
J. C. Nottingham

A   This is one of those it-all-depends type answers. The main determining factor is file format, if you save scanned images as 'bitmap' files (extension *.bmp) you can reckon on 2 to 3 Mb per picture. If you use the far more economical JPEG (extension *.jpg) format, which uses data compression to reduce the amount of space required, then the size of files will be reduced by a factor of 10 or so, to 300 Kb per picture, say, without any significant loss of quality. So, for example, a thousand JPEG image files would occupy up to 300 Mb of disk space; the same number of bitmaps would need around 3 gigabytes.

Hidden Fax

Q   I recall reading that Windows 98 has the Microsoft fax programs, but they are hidden in a remote file. Can you tell me what the file name is? *I. C. via e-mail*

A   It is on the CD-ROM, go to Tools > Oldwin95 > Intnl and click on Wms.exe and Awfax.exe to install the Windows Messaging and Fax components.

CHAPTER 8

Building your own web site

You might not believe it, but creating your own Internet web site is easy.

Shortly after your first successful sessions exploring the Internet you will probably want to build your own web site. Have a go; it's much easier than you think! The volume and diversity of information is what makes the Internet such a valuable and important resource. You almost certainly have something to contribute, or sell, but where do you start?

You don't need any specialist knowledge or skills to construct a web site. If you have Windows 95 or 98 and a web browser on your PC you already possess all the software needed, though it will be a lot easier if you have a word processor like Microsoft Word 97, or one of the many web authoring packages now available.

It's not expensive either; there are some excellent freeware and shareware programs included on magazine cover-mount CD-ROMs, or available for the cost of a download from numerous sites around the web, for example:

- Arachnophalia, www.arachnoid.com
- HomeSite, www.allaire.com
- HotDog Express, www.sausage.com
- PaintShop Pro, www.jasc.com

Most Internet service providers (ISPs) provide subscribers with several megabytes of free web space; however, if you need a more permanent and controlled presence on the web you should consider paying for space and using a specialist agency to create and maintain your site.

Although not essential, it's worth knowing just a little about how an Internet web site is put together. As you will have discovered, it is possible to move around a document or site, or jump to another web site by simply clicking your PC mouse pointer on coloured and underlined

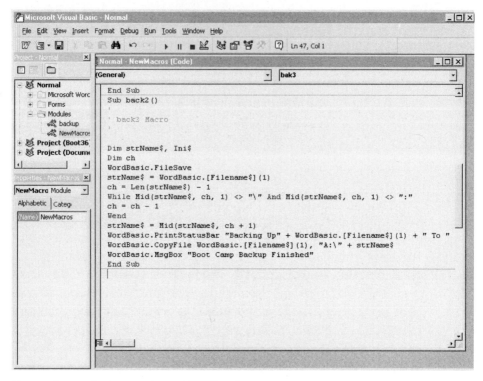

Use your browser to view a web page's HTML code

text or 'buttons'. They're called links and behind the scenes, embedded in the pages, are hidden instructions, written in a code called HTML or HyperText Mark-up Language. They tell the browser software what to do and where to go.

HTML is based on simple text commands. It's not complicated, but it can be a bit long-winded to write and check the codes manually. You can easily see them for yourself when you're viewing a web page if you're using Internet Explorer or Netscape Navigator. In Explorer right click on some text and Windows 95/98 Notepad will appear, showing all the codes and copy. If you're using Netscape highlight the text then go to the View menu and click on Document Source. The good news is you don't need to learn HTML right now, but it might come in handy later on if you want to incorporate some of the special features that you may have seen on other web sites.

The key to a successful web site is planning. Before you go any further decide what information you want your site to contain, how you want it to look in terms of layout and illustrations and how it is going to work. In other words, how the various pages connect to one another. Try roughing out a few ideas on paper first. There are very few hard and fast rules; the best place to pick up the dos and don'ts is by looking at how others do it and learn from their mistakes. You can get some good advice and a crash course in how not to design a web site by visiting http://www.webpagesthatsuck.com.

The most important element of any web site is the first page or 'Home page', the one that your visitors will see when they arrive. From there it should be possible to get to any other part of the site, and back to your home page, so plan your links carefully. Keep your introduction copy short, relevant and above all interesting. Everyone likes a freebie, so if you've something to give away – be it an essential nugget of information, software, product or service – make sure it's prominently mentioned on your home page. Feedback is essential – you want to know what people think about your site – so don't forget to include your e-mail address somewhere on the home page. Avoid complicated graphics or illustrations that may take a long time to download; anything that takes longer than 5 to 10 seconds to appear can be a real turn-off and your visitors might just decide to leave before they've reached the good bits. You may want to direct visitors to other related sites so compile a list of Internet addresses and make sure they work on your browser.

Now you are ready to use your word processor to write the main text. When you have finished double-check spelling and grammar, then check it again, or get someone else to read it through. Spelling mistakes, especially big ones – on headlines and banners – look incredibly amateurish and reflect very badly on you. Finally gather together the illustrations you'll be using. You can edit them using programs such as PaintShop Pro, and save them in JPEG (for photographs) and GIF (for graphics) file formats, ready for inclusion in your Web pages.

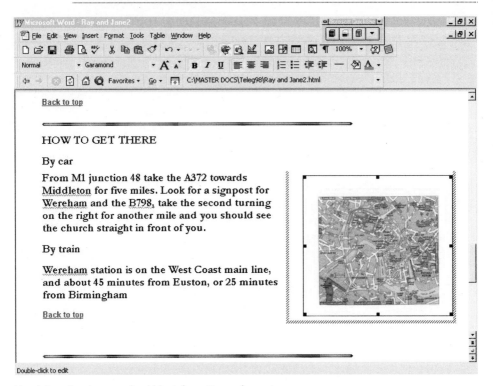

Your Internet web pages should be informative and easy to use

Projects

BUILDING A WEB SITE

If you have a reasonably up-to-date Windows 95 PC with Internet access and Microsoft Word 97 you can create your own Internet web site quickly and easily. Graphics software such as PaintShop Pro, and a scanner or digital camera will come in useful too, but you can get started without them.

It's a good idea to assemble all of the components (text and picture files) in a single folder, it saves time and stops things getting lost. While you're at it create a second folder, for finished web pages.

The subject for our example web site is a family wedding. The intention would be to set it up well ahead of the big day, to give friends and family at home and abroad the opportunity to participate. It will feature a timetable, photos and potted biographies of the happy couple. There will be a present list, maps of how to get to the church and reception plus a message board for e-mail greetings. After the wedding, the site can be used to feature a gallery of photographs and visitors can order copies.

We're using the easiest possible method, which is to modify a ready-made web page template. This technique is common to a lot of commercial and shareware web authoring programs and a key feature in the latest versions of Microsoft Word, which is bundled with a lot of new PCs; so to keep things simple that's what we'll be using. Start with the Web page Wizard by selecting 'New' on the 'File' drop-down menu; click on it and choose a style. Don't be surprised if they look

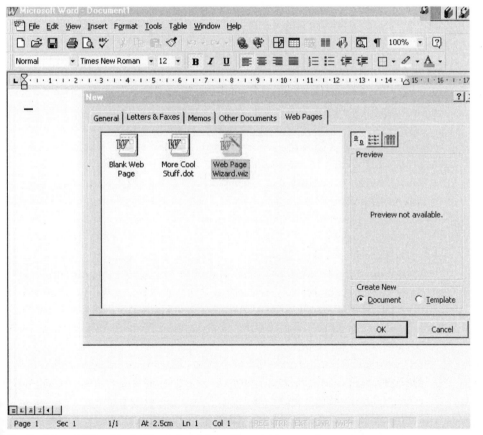

Use the Internet Wizard to decide on the style and layout of your web pages

familiar, countless thousands of web sites have been based on these and similar templates.

Personal Home Page is one of the best options for first-timers; it allows you to put everything onto one page and it's the ideal layout for our modest 'Wed Site'. For larger sites with a lot of text and illustrations it's better to use multiple pages, to reduce the download time. Next select a background, choose one of the defaults, even if you don't much care for them, you can easily change it later, or create your own.

Before you go any further it's a good idea to spend a few minutes familiarising yourself with how the site works. Click on the coloured, underlined hypertext links, and see where they lead. Now you can make a start on the copy by replacing the sample text. Begin with the banner at the top of the page then move on to a sub-heading and a short introduction paragraph. You can key it in, straight to the page or import pre-prepared copy from another file, using the copy and paste facility. If you wish you can change typefaces and font sizes by highlighting text blocks and using the appropriate buttons on the toolbar. Don't get too carried away though, exotic styles can be difficult to read and you can waste a lot of time fiddling around, when you should be getting on with the job. When you're happy with the first few lines go to the File drop-down menu, select Save As, give your new web site a name and put it into the web page folder. Get into the habit of saving your work every 15 minutes or so, just in case.

Step two is to modify the links. Work your way down the list, changing the wording of each underlined hyperlink and inserting the linked text block. Do them one at a time or you could get into a muddle. When you've completed one or two links it's a good idea to test the page, to make sure it is working properly. Save the document and click on the Web Page Preview button on the toolbar or open your Internet browser (use the Open or Open File command on the File menu). What you now see is the actual page as it will appear when it has been downloaded from the Internet. Try out the links and if everything is okay, go back and continue inputting the new copy. Finish off by inserting any addresses you might want to include to other web pages – MS Word should automatically recognise them as web addresses, with an appropriate colour change and underline. Don't forget to put in your own e-mail address and any other essential information. Lastly, delete any unwanted sample text that has been left behind.

Step three is to drop in the artwork. If you haven't already done so, ensure the image files are in the correct format – JPEG for photographs and GIF for graphics. Decide roughly where you want an image to go by inserting a flashing cursor with the left mouse button. Go to the Insert menu, select 'Picture' and then 'From File' options to open your first image. Check the 'Float Over Text' box – this will make it easier to move the picture around on the page – click on OK and the picture will appear on your web page. Unless you have already reduced the size of the image it will probably need resizing – use one of the corner squares – then drag and drop it into position. Pictures and graphics can make

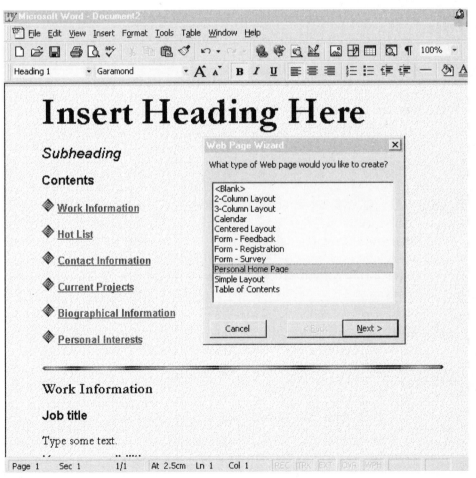

It couldn't be easier, just choose the background and styles then key in your text

unexpected changes to your layout that may not show up on the make-up screen, so check how it is looking on your browser from time to time.

When the text and pictures are in place and the page has been saved, you can spend some time playing around with the design elements. Add borders to pictures and decorative lines to break up the page (Horizontal Lines on the Insert menu) or try modifying the background; there's a good assortment of fill-in colours and textures filed under 'Background' on the Format drop-down menu. You will find even more patterns, textures, graphics, animations and templates, plus many useful web page features on Microsoft's Site Builder Gallery (http://www.microsoft.com/gallery/default.asp) – they're yours for the cost of a download. Give the spelling and grammar one last run-through, re-check the links and save your page. It really is that easy!

GETTING YOUR SITE ONTO THE NET

Now we come to the tricky part, getting your site up and running on the Internet. It's tricky, not because it's difficult, but there are just so many different ways of doing it.

The first step is to find someone to host your site. You can either pay for it – the best option if you're using it to sell something or promote a service – or you can take up one of the many offers of free space that are available. Free space usually comes with strings attached, but that needn't be a problem: in fact it can work to your advantage if your site is devoted to helping others or is of a charitable nature. Shared single-subject sites are a useful resource and often a lot easier for visitors to find. To see if there are any appropriate servers, access one of the main search engines (Yahoo, Alta Vista, Lycos, Infoseek etc.) enter 'free web space' plus suitable key words ('Scouting', 'disability', 'childcare', etc.) into the search field and see what comes up.

Internet Service Providers (ISPs) usually give subscribers an allocation of free space. Use it if you've got it, but read the small print; you might find there are restrictions on what you can and cannot publish. They're usually reluctant to let you use it for commercial purposes, or anything they deem socially or politically unacceptable. The other problem with free space is the ISP can pull the plug at any time, and they're not obliged to warn you, or tell you why. The same applies to

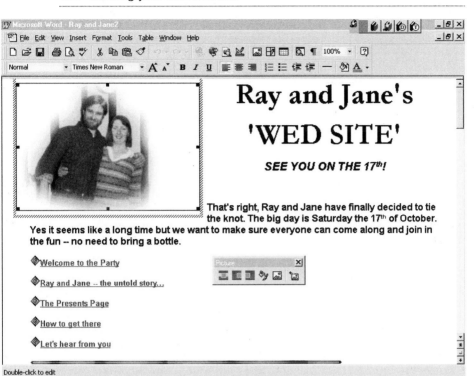

The example 'Wed' site contains all the information guests and
well-wishers will need for the big day

servers who provide free space in return for allowing them to put advertising on your pages. You will have little or no control over advertising content – you could end up with an ad for a burger restaurant on your web site for vegetarian recipes – moreover you have no say in how long they will host your site.

Don't be put off by the fact that a host server is overseas. This is an irrelevance on the Internet and it may well be that your visitors will get faster access if the company is well connected to the network.

However, for the purposes of this exercise we'll assume that you're going to use your allocation of free space, provided by your ISP. The precise method of uploading a web site onto a host server varies enormously so you will have to do a little research. Access your ISP's free web site tutorial, which will outline the exact procedures. It should also tell you how the all-important URL (uniform resource locator) or addresses for your site is allocated. In some cases you may need to change file names on your web site in order to conform to their system. They may also advise you to add extra hypertext links or HTML code, but this is a very simple procedure, involving typing a line or two of text and symbols onto your pages. Remember that your web site must contain all necessary files, including text, images and anything else that visitors may want to access.

After your site has been uploaded make a careful note of the URL and log off. Log on again then try accessing your site. When the page appears re-check all of the links. If there are any mistakes return to the original files on your PC, make the appropriate changes and go through the upload procedure again. This will overwrite the existing site. You can use this method to update the site as often as necessary.

Now the site is operational it is time to publicise it by making sure that as many search engines as possible list it, or can find it. Once again there are lots of different methods. You can do it manually, by accessing each search engine in turn and looking for their Submit Form link; however, since there are literally hundreds of search engines, this could take a while. The alternative is to use a program to do it for you. Web site registration utilities like SoftSpider(http://softspider.com) and Add Web 2.01 (http://www.cyberspacehq.com) are available in shareware form. Usually the shareware version will only register your site with a limited number of search engines, but they tend to be the most popular ones. If you want to register with more you will have to pay. Nevertheless, they are all very simple to use. Just enter the details of your site, the URL, a short description of what it contains and some keywords.

You can also register your site with multiple search engines on-line. The best known submission sites are Add Me (www.adme.com) – they'll send your details to 34 search engines for free – and Submit-it (http://www.submit-it.com), who currently deal with over 400 search sites. Links to and from other related sites are a very useful way of attracting visitors, so contact those sites and offer to put a link on your site in exchange for them carrying yours.

And that is everything you need to know to create a web site and publish it on the Internet. Needless to say you can make it a great deal more complicated, and there are countless embellishments you can incorporate into your site. There are literally hundreds of books and Internet sites (such as http://www.geocities.com) offering further guidance, and hopefully you'll receive plenty of feedback from your visitors. However, the point to bear in mind is that the basic principles are easily mastered, if you've managed to get to grips with a word processor, you can do it!

Q&A # Real world problems

Digital downside

Q Still photographs can be incorporated into personal Web sites easily but what about digital video? Could you please suggest any drawbacks that you can think of to incorporate digital video clips into a web site. The dilemma is: should I buy a digital still camera or spend extra money for a digital video camera with the facility for taking still pictures as well!
N. F. W. via e-mail

A By all means buy a digital camcorder for making home video movies and all models have a facility for taking video stills as well, but it would be a complete waste of money if used solely for making video clips for web pages. Any analogue camcorder (VHS-C or 8 mm or high-band variants S-VHS-C and Hi8) will more than suffice. Digital camcorders are capable of near broadcast-quality recordings but the Internet can only carry jerky low-resolution moving images, for the moment at least.

   The principle advantage digital camcorders have over their analogue counterparts is the ease with which recordings can be downloaded onto a PC, using a FireWire or IEEE 1394 interface card. This means the data recorded on the camcorder tape remains in the digital domain and doesn't have to go through so many damaging conversion processes, before ending up on the PC's hard disk drive. Digital recordings can be edited on the PC far more efficiently than other means and replayed back to tape, with no loss of quality. However, this is an expensive business with digital interface cards costing £250 plus and 'desk-top video' PCs need very fast processors, lots of memory and massive hard disk drives. In contrast you can use almost any Pentium class PC to make video clips (suitable for web use) from footage recorded on an analogue camcorder. All you need is a video capture card or 'grabber', such as ArcSoft 'Zipshot' or Iomega 'Buz' or even an inexpensive TV card, such as the Miro TV, all of which come with simple AVI (audio video interleaved) editing software.

Domain decision

Q   I am thinking of setting up a family web site. My ISP has given me 20 Mb of free web space but the address is really long and may be difficult for others to find. Is it worth paying extra for a 'domain' name, so friends and family can easily get to the site?
E. L. via e-mail

A   Having your own domain name will certainly shorten the URL or web address, but in addition to the registration fee – anywhere from around £50 upwards – there's the annual maintenance fee (about £100) and there may be hidden extras for forwarding e-mail. The extra costs make sense if you are using your web site for business or commercial purposes, but for personal use it is questionable.

Picture this

Q   I am planning to buy a digital still camera so that I can take pictures that I can incorporate on a web site my wife and I am planning to start. What type of camera do you recommend, and will I be able to use it to photograph documents – birth certificates etc. – that we want to show on the site?
H. A. via e-mail

A   Digital still cameras are wonderful and ideal for taking pictures for web pages but you might want to hold off buying one for a while in preference to a scanner. A scanner will let you scan in documents for your web pages, as well as old photographs and more recent ones, taken using a normal camera. Digital cameras are not really good enough for capturing fine print on documents; in fact the only real advantages of a digital camera is minimal processing cost and speed, but with one-hour processing available in almost every high street and supermarket even that's questionable. A budget scanner, on the other hand, sells for around £50 and in addition to image processing they can be used for faxing, colour copying and OCR (optical character recognition) text reading.

Today's the day

Q   Do you know of any web addresses from which I could find information on world events, political, sporting, humorous, social etc., for any given date? The date could be by the year or by the actual day, for example 1968 or January 12th 1982.
   A. S. via e-mail

A   There certainly is – lots of them, in fact. They've even got their own home page. Check out the links at Today In History: http://www.request.net/history/today-in-history/index.htm.

Duty calls

Q   Please could you tell me if there is any duty rota software currently available for use on a PC? I work on a busy surgical ward that employs 30 people and it is necessary to determine the correct skill mix of staff. I know that some hospital trusts have a facility available through their mainframes, but colleagues and friends have drawn a blank on stand-alone applications.
   S. L. via e-mail

A   A quick search on the Internet using 'duty roster' as search keywords threw up several promising sites. You might like to begin with a program called Shift Easy from Go Safety Ltd. Its site (http://www.gosafety.aust.com/p113.htm) includes a downloadable demonstration copy.

Shock of the new

Q   A web site I visited recently asked me if I wanted to accept something called 'Shockwave'. Please advise if this is 'free' and what should I do next?
P. K. via e-mail

A   It can be a bit unnerving when a web site asks if it can download files or programs onto your machine. You are wise to be cautious, but usually there's nothing to worry about. A lot of web sites use fancy graphics and animations, in order for you to view them your browser program needs to be upgraded, and this is what will happen if you click on OK. It is free and it should only take a few moments, after which you will be able to see the site in all its glory. If you choose not to install the upgrade you can still access the site and read the text content.

CHAPTER 9 **Easier access**

Don't let your PC control your life - make it work for you, not the other way around!

Like it or lump it seems to have been the attitude of computer and software developers since the earliest days of the PC. Systems for the office and home have been mostly designed for a notional Mr and Ms average, sound in wind and limb with a full complement of working eyes and ears. Numerous common disabilities mean PCs are difficult or even impossible to use. However, the two areas that cause the most problems are input devices, such as keyboards and mice, and video displays.

Windows 98 and, to a slightly lesser extent, Windows 95, has a number of 'Accessibility' features that can help make life easier for those with a range of mobility or visual impairments. However, they are not normally loaded by default during a routine installation. The first step therefore is to install the necessary utilities from the Windows CD-ROM. From the Start menu go to Settings then Control Panel and Add/Remove programs. Select the Windows Set-up tab; check the Accessibility box then follow the instructions.

Once installed a new Accessibility icon will appear in Control Panel. The basic options – common to both Windows 95 and 98 – cover keyboard actions, visual indicators for sounds, high contrast settings for the display and a way to divert mouse movement commands to the keyboard. Additionally Windows 98 has a very useful screen magnifier and a configuration Wizard that helps users adapt Windows to their specific needs.

The keyboard features are 'Sticky Keys', 'Filter Keys', and 'Toggle Keys'. Sticky Keys makes it easier to use keyboard commands or shortcuts that require the Shift, Ctrl or Alt key to be held down while pressing

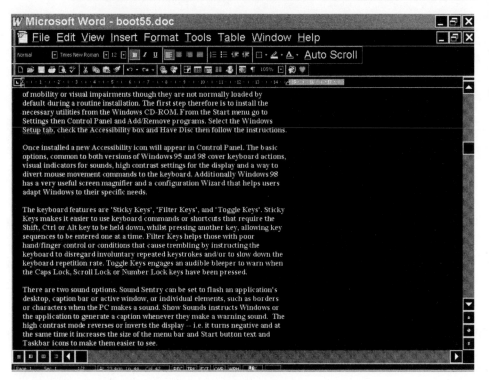

of mobility or visual impairments though they are not normally loaded by default during a routine installation. The first step therefore is to install the necessary utilities from the Windows CD-ROM. From the Start menu go to Settings then Control Panel and Add/Remove programs. Select the Windows Setup tab, check the Accessibility box and Have Disc then follow the instructions.

Once installed a new Accessibility icon will appear in Control Panel. The basic options, common to both versions of Windows 95 and 98 cover keyboard actions, visual indicators for sounds, high contrast settings for the display and a way to divert mouse movement commands to the keyboard. Additionally Windows 98 has a very useful screen magnifier and a configuration Wizard that helps users adapt Windows to their specific needs.

The keyboard features are 'Sticky Keys', 'Filter Keys', and 'Toggle Keys'. Sticky Keys makes it easier to use keyboard commands or shortcuts that require the Shift, Ctrl or Alt key to be held down, whilst pressing another key, allowing key sequences to be entered one at a time. Filter Keys helps those with poor hand/finger control or conditions that cause trembling by instructing the keyboard to disregard involuntary repeated keystrokes and/or to slow down the keyboard repetition rate. Toggle Keys engages an audible bleeper to warn when the Caps Lock, Scroll Lock or Number Lock keys have been pressed.

There are two sound options. Sound Sentry can be set to flash an application's desktop, caption bar or active window, or individual elements, such as borders or characters when the PC makes a sound. Show Sounds instructs Windows or the application to generate a caption whenever they make a warning sound. The high contrast mode reverses or inverts the display -- i.e. it turns negative and at the same time it increases the size of the menu bar and Start button text and Taskbar icons to make them easier to see.

Text legibility is dramatically improved using the High Contrast colour scheme

another key; when activated key sequences can be entered one at a time. Filter Keys helps those with poor hand/finger control or conditions that cause trembling by instructing the keyboard to disregard involuntary or repeated keystrokes and to slow down the keyboard repetition rate. Toggle Keys engages an audible bleeper to warn when the Caps Lock, Scroll Lock or Number Lock keys have been pressed.

There are two sound options. Sound Sentry can be set to flash an application's desktop, caption bar or active window, or individual elements, such as borders or characters, when the PC makes a sound. Show Sounds instructs Windows or the application to generate text captions whenever it makes a warning sound. On the display tab there is High Contrast mode which reverses or inverts the display – i.e. it turns the image negative and at the same time it increases the size of the menu bar and Start button text and Taskbar icons, to make them easier to see. This works very well on word processors and spreadsheets and is also worth trying if you're having trouble seeing the display due to reflections from windows or overhead lighting.

MouseKeys is intended for those with restricted hand movement, but who can still use a keyboard. This feature transfers mouse control to the numeric keypad on the right side of the keyboard. Many recent Windows keyboards already have the direction arrows printed on the numeric keys, with the mouse buttons assigned to surrounding keys.

The Screen Magnifier is included with Windows 98 as standard though again it is not installed by default. It is an option on the Accessibility menu in Control Panel or it can be found by typing 'Screen Magnify' in the Help Index. When it is running the screen is split into two sections; the horizontal divider can be moved to alter the size of the upper viewing window. The lower window shows the application you are using. The magnification factor can be adjusted between 2× and 9×; the viewing screen can be set to follow the mouse pointer,

The Screen Magnifier in Windows 98 allows you to see your program close up, between 2x and 9x normal size

keyboard focus or text editor. From the Magnifier dialogue box it is also possible to switch the image to a negative display and select the High Contrast display scheme. If you are using an older version of Windows, or another operating system there are lots of third-party screen magnifier programs, including some excellent freeware and shareware utilities that can be downloaded from the Internet. The Screen Magnifier Homepage (presented in a large easy to read type-face) is a good place to begin: http://www.plex.nl/~pverhoe/main2.html.

People who are totally blind or have very limited vision have the option to use various types of non-visual media. Voice synthesiser systems that translate text and program control information into speech have proven successful. Refreshable Braille displays provide the same kind of feedback – about what is happening on the screen – this time in a tactile form. The Royal National Institute for the Blind web site (http://www.rnib.org.uk) contains a wealth of information and links for visually impaired PC users.

For those who have problems with a standard QWERTY keyboard there are many alternatives, including on-screen keyboards, specialist designs that can be used single-handed, models with extra large keys, keys embossed with Braille characters or customised to meet the needs of a specific disability. It's worth talking to the society, association or charity linked to the sufferer's particular condition for more detailed advice.

Some users may find a trackball is a better alternative to a mouse or keyboard. It is also worth experimenting with the mouse motion settings. These can be found by clicking on the Mouse icon in Control Panel. While you are there check the various different kinds of pointers available, there are larger and coloured versions that can be easier to see.

THE POWER OF SPEECH

You might be interested to know that this first paragraph was written using a highly respected speech recognition program. Almost any recent Windows PC can be programmed to recognise and respond to the user's voice, converting speech into text, for writing letters, composing e-mails or faxes.

It took a little over 10 minutes to enter those 50 or so words, which is why the rest of this piece is being typed on a keyboard. In the past few

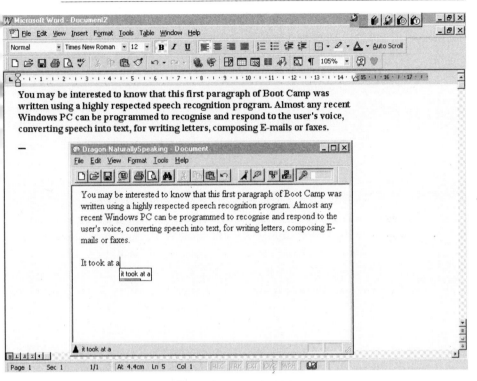

Voice recognition programs like Naturally Speaking enter text into a
dedicated window first, before the file is exported to a word processor

years speech recognition software has improved in leaps and bounds,
but even the very best systems still require a lot of patience and hard
work to get them up to anything like a useful speed. In the early stages
it's not much faster than one-fingered, hunt-and-peck typing and it
all goes to pot if you catch a cold, lose your voice or work in a noisy
environment.

But what if you cannot type, either through physical disability or a
keen dislike/fear of the keyboard? In that case, voice recognition is a
practical way of getting your words into a PC. However, do not expect
instant hands-free computing. Even the fastest and most efficient voice
recognition programs have to go through a long-winded training process,
to learn the user's voice before they can achieve worthwhile accuracy.
Moreover, some speech recognition systems make heavy weather of
menu commands and program controls so you could still end up using
the keyboard and/or mouse for a lot of routine operations.

Although several voice recognition programs are available that work on older and slower PCs, for the best results you will need a fairly recent and speedy Pentium or Pentium class multimedia machine. Other basic requirements are Windows 95 or 98, at least 16 Mb of RAM and upwards of 60 Mb of free hard disk space. The PC should have an up-to-date soundcard, plus you will need a microphone or headset with a boom mike. A headset-type microphone is preferable as these are less sensitive to background noises and the performance is usually more consistent.

Installing a voice recognition program from CD-ROM normally takes only a few minutes, and that's when the fun begins. The program's first action is to go into a set-up routine, to measure background noise levels then test and adjust the sensitivity of the microphone. The amount of vocal training these packages require varies quite a lot. The initial session can easily last more than half an hour, and most of them need continual training to maintain accuracy.

The programs also work in slightly different ways. The majority have

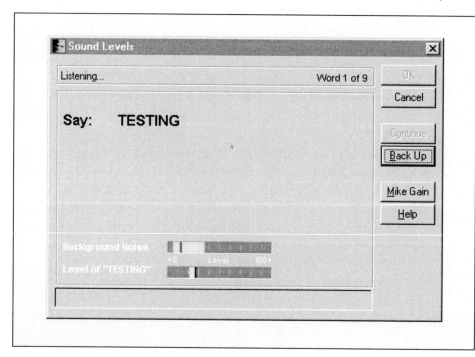

'Testing Testing'. Setting the background noise and microphone levels in Kurzweil Voice

the option (though not always included as standard) to enter text directly onto the page of your chosen word processor, as you speak. Others have their own text window. Once a file has been created and corrected it is exported to an application, such as a word processor, fax program or Internet e-mail window.

Even after a program has been fully trained it is important to remember to speak clearly and slowly using a consistently natural voice and accent, or at least the same voice that you used when setting up the program. And above all, keep calm! Even the best programs make frequent mistakes and there is a natural tendency to raise the pitch of the voice in frustration, which makes it even harder for the program to follow what you're saying.

Voice recognition is a fast moving technology with huge vested interests in getting it to work properly. There is absolutely no doubt that within a very few years we'll all be chatting merrily to our PCs and the keyboard will become obsolete. The bottom line is that at the present state of development it is a very worthwhile aid for those who cannot use a keyboard. For everyone else, with fully functioning hands and fingers, voice recognition ranks as an interesting novelty – it's quite spooky to see words appear on the screen as they are spoken but if you're looking for an easy ride forget it. There's a good chance you'll end up expending more time and effort than if you simply learned to type.

CONTACTS

Dragon Dictate/Naturally Speaking, Dragon Systems (01242) 678575, http://www.dragonsys.com

ViaVoice/Simply speaking/Voice Type, IBM (0990) 727272, www.ibm.com

Microsoft http://www.research.microsoft.com/research/srg/,http://officeupdate.microsoft.com/downloadcatalog/dldword.htm

Kurzweil Voice/VoicePad Pro, Talking Technologies 0171-602 4107, www.talk-systems.com

Q&A Real world problems

Speech therapy

Q   Now well into my seventies, I am very deaf, a problem originating from when I flew noisy Wellington bombers during WW2. In spite of two powerful hearing aids, I'm afraid my wife and I have been reduced to going to sign language classes in order that I can respond to simple questions, such as 'Would you like another slice of cake?' Is there such as thing as a small instrument that converts speech into text? Meanwhile, I see that a number of software companies have produced programs for dictating into word processors. I am contemplating purchasing a small laptop, which I can have by my armchair, a microphone (radio mike?) for my wife and a useful speech program, so we can communicate.
D. B. Chelmsford

A   A 'black box' speech-to-text processor is technically possible, but a practical and affordable device is still some way off. PC speech recognition packages like Dragon Naturally Speaking (the basic version sells for around £40) can convert continuous speech into words on a PC screen and is definitely worth trying. However, even this leading-edge product is far from perfect. It will involve a fair amount of 'training' in order for the software to reliably translate your wife's words into text but if you both persevere there's no reason why it shouldn't work.

Pregnant pause

Q   Is it dangerous for a pregnant woman to sit at a computer screen with other screens in close proximity? Can this cause a miscarriage or damage a foetus?
H. E. Twickenham

A   The most recent research indicates that there is no link between miscarriages or birth defects and using a VDU during pregnancy. However, some experts have suggested that stress and worry – prompted by media reports and scare stories about the safety of VDUs – could be a factor in some cases. Modern PC monitors are subject to strict regulations and the levels of ionising radiation they emit is now at a very low level, below that of most televisions. Emissions from monitors can be reduced still further with specially designed shields or by using LCD (liquid crystal display) type monitors. It is impossible to say categorically that there are no risks. If you are concerned, you should discuss the matter with your employer or whoever in your company is responsible for health and safety matters. The Health and Safety Executive (HSE) has prepared a useful pamphlet on the subject, it can be viewed on the internet at http://www.open.gov.uk/hse/pubns/indg36.htm, or you can obtain a copy from the HSE by phoning (01787) 881165 and requesting document INDG36, 'Working with VDUs'.

Leftist tendency

Q   Is there such a thing as an ambidextrous mouse for a PC? My seven year-old daughter is left-handed and so we have set the mouse to be left-handed. My three year-old son is right handed and now wants to 'have a go'. Can we set the mouse to suit them both without having to change the set-up each time?
V. D. via e-mail

A   Why not put a desktop shortcut to the Mouse set-up utility in Control Panel. That would help to speed things up? Simply left click on the icon and select Create Shortcut. You can also put the shortcut onto the Start menu by dragging the icon onto the Start button.

Laser on the loose

Q   I recently purchased a Panasonic LF-D101 DVD RAM drive. Having installed it I started to read the manual. The first section that I came across warned me, amongst other things, 'not to get my eyes close to the panel opening door in order to avoid exposure to invisible laser radiation'. Within the tower set up I have I can occasionally see a green light through the slit between the DVD RAM drive and the front panel blanking plate which hides the hard drive unit in the space above. Do you know if there is any danger posed by looking at this green light?

Also, is there any way of assessing whether the DVD RAM drive 'leaks' invisible radiation to the areas where I am usually sitting.
D. P. via e-mail

A   The green light you're seeing is the 'activity' indicator LED, probably on the front of the nearby hard disk drive. It is perfectly harmless. As the instruction book says, the laser used inside the DVD emits invisible light, even if it was 'leaking' you wouldn't see it. However, it is highly unlikely any laser light could escape. Manufacturers go to a lot of trouble to make sure it stays safely inside the case. Moreover, all CD and DVD decks have safety interlocks that prevent the laser from operating when the drive door or loading tray is open.

Sound advice

Q   I have recently had some problems with my PC, which have now been corrected. However, I am now unable to alter the volume on my PC, as the volume control option is no longer there. Can you please tell me how to get it back?
V. E. via e-mail

A   Go to: Start > Settings > Control Panel > Multimedia, and on the Audio tab check the box marked 'Show Volume Control on the Task Bar'.

Yank keys

Q   My @ sign prints " (quotes), and quotes prints @. My pound sign prints # (hash), and my hash key prints \ (backslash). Nothing prints a pound sign. How can I change the keyboard settings so that I get what I press?
D. W. via e-mail

A   The most likely explanation is that the Windows keyboard configuration is set to the wrong language. It was probably left on the English (American) default when Windows was installed. Go to Start > Settings > Control Panel > Keyboard, double click the icon and select the Language tab. If, as seems likely, it is set to something other than English (British) change it by clicking on the Add button and follow the instructions.

CHAPTER 10 **Upgrading your PC**

You can make your PC run faster and more efficiently, it's easy!

Before we begin, a few words of warning. If electronic gadgets keel over and die if you so much as look at them, or you always seem to have bits left over when you take something apart, please skip this chapter. On the other hand, if you can wire up a three-pin plug or change a fuse without electrocuting yourself, upgrading and adding extra bits to your PC should be a breeze.

CD WRITERS

You probably don't want to know this, but all the programs and data stored in your computer reside in a microscopically thin magnetic coating on thin metal discs spinning at several thousand revolutions per minute. All it takes is a single speck of dust, a sharp knock or a virus to destroy all of the information held on your PC's hard disk drive. Fortunately it doesn't happen very often, and you are fully protected against viruses (aren't you?), but suppose the worst did happen, how would you fare?

If all of your non-replaceable data is safely backed up then it need be no more than an inconvenience. Mass storage devices are so cheap nowadays there's no excuse not to protect your computer against hard disk failure or corruption and it also makes it easier to archive or swap large files between PCs. Of course you can save data on floppy discs – the 1.44 Mb capacity is sufficient for important system files, a few documents or one or two images, but far too small to be of use with today's video and multimedia applications. Data can be compressed, to make more efficient use of the floppy's limited storage space and Windows 95/98 has a useful backup utility builtin (My Computer > right click

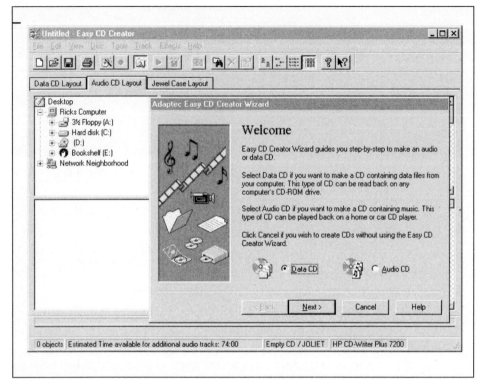

A CD writer allows you to create data or music CDs with a few simple
mouse clicks

drive C: > Properties > Tools). But there are simpler solutions.

Basically there are three hardware options: magnetic tape, magnetic
disk, and optical disk, we'll look at each one in turn. Magnetic tape
systems have two distinct advantages; they are cheap and they hold
enormous amounts of data. The cheapest tape-based backup system
is the Danmere Backer which sells for less than £40 and can download
the contents of a hard disk drive on to a 3-hour video tape costing a
couple of pounds. More advanced tape systems such as the Hewlett
Packard Colorado, Segate Travan or Iomega Ditto, use dedicated data
cartridges; drives cost upwards of £140 and can hold 5 or more gigabytes of compressed data. However, all tape-based recording systems
are slow and because data is stored in a 'linear' form – along a length
of tape – it can take a long time to retrieve a particular file or group
of files. Since there are many different types of magnetic tape cartridge

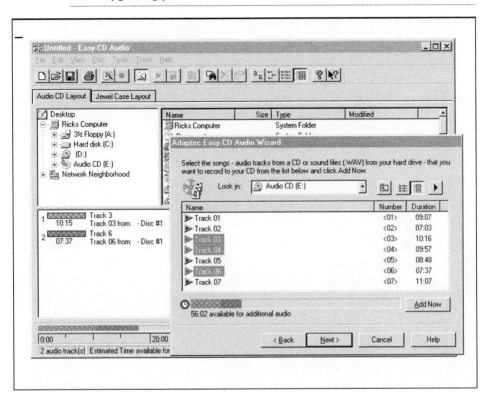

You can compile your own custom music CDs by picking selected tracks

or cassette file swapping is restricted to other PCs using the same system.

There are also lots of different magnetic disk formats on the market. You could even install a second hard disk drive, though it won't be much use if the PC is stolen or damaged in a fire. Removable drives solve that problem, but a far more convenient solution is a high-capacity floppy disk system, like Zip, Jaz or LS120. Zip disks hold 100 Mb of uncompressed data (a 250 Mb zip drive is also available), whilst its larger cousin the Jaz has a 2 Gb capacity. LS120 disks hold 120 Mb, the drives can also read and write to 3.5-inch floppies and like Zip drives they are relatively inexpensive. Basic internal Zip and LS120 drives cost around £80 and the discs sell for £8 to £15 each when brought singly. The recently introduced Zip 250 Mb model costs £170. Jaz drives are a little dearer at just under £300 while the disks are quite pricey at £60.

File swapping is still a problem unless all of the PCs in question are fitted with, or connected to compatible drive mechanisms.

Optical and magneto-optical disk recorders are now an increasingly affordable alternative to magnetic media and are ideal for archiving large picture or video files. The cost of recordable CD-ROM drives has plummeted in the past year and the newly introduced DVD-RAM format is not far behind. However, a CD-ROM writer is still the best option for most PC users and home-made disks can be read on any PC with a CD-ROM drive, so file swapping is not an issue. In most instances the new drive is installed alongside the existing CD-ROM, so you end up with two drives on your PC, which is quite handy if you routinely need to access more than one disk.

CD-ROM writers can now be bought for as little as £120 and blank discs that can hold up to 650 Mb of data cost from just £1 each. In fact there are two types of recordable CD-ROM disk, CD-R disks can only be recorded once, files can be added at intervals but once the disk is full that's it. CD-RW (read-write) disks cost around £10 to £15 each but they can be erased and re-written many times. Recordable CD-ROMs are not quite as robust as their non-recordable counterparts, but properly stored the data on them should be safe for several decades. Most recordable CD-ROM drives can do other tricks, such as duplicate data CD-ROMs and copy or create audio CD compilations of your favourite tracks.

Projects

INSTALLING A CD WRITER

Installing an internal CD-ROM writer takes only a few minutes. The mechanism slots into a spare drive next to the existing CD-ROM drive and plugs into the same cable (there's usually a spare connector) and a spare power lead. The set-up software on CD-ROM is read from the first drive and Windows 95/98 automatically installs the new hardware. Once the new drive is up and running it becomes a second CD-ROM with its own drive letter. A simple utility program supplied with the drive prepares disks and files for recording using familiar Windows

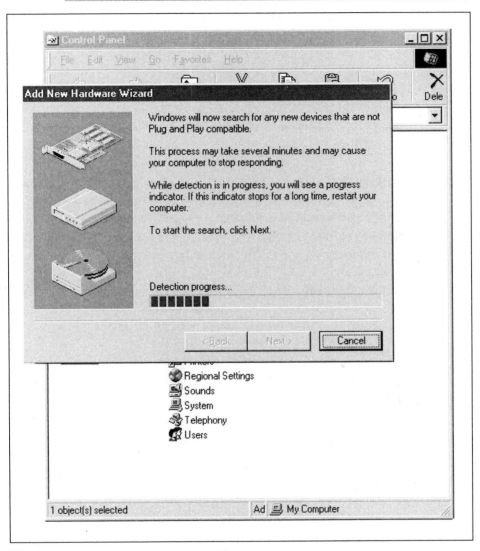

Windows makes it easy to install a new item of hardware

file copying methods. Backing up 650 Mb of data on a typical 2× speed drive takes only a few minutes but it could save you days or weeks of disruption!

ADDING MORE MEMORY

A memory upgrade is the easiest, quickest and most cost-effective improvement you can make to your PC. The memory in question is known as RAM or Random Access Memory. It's a collection of micro-chips that the computer uses to temporarily store programs and data which it needs to access quickly and frequently. RAM capacity is measured in megabytes, a Windows 95 or 98 PC will operate with just 8 Mb but 16 Mb is considered the safe minimum, 32 Mb is optimum for most types of home and business software; 64 Mb is recommended as the starting point for PCs running graphic intensive applications or fast action games.

RAM chips are mounted on small strip-like modules that plug into sockets on the large printed circuit board or 'motherboard' inside your PC's system box. The modules are designed to be easy to fit, and im-possible to insert the wrong way around. If you're properly prepared, the whole job shouldn't take more than 15 to 20 minutes.

Increasing RAM capacity can make a dramatic difference to the speed of your applications. You will experience fewer crashes and it may even extend the useful life of your machine. It is usual to increase PC memory by a factor of 2, 4, 8, 16 etc., up to the capacity of the mother-board. This also happens to be a very good time to do it since memory cards are cheap and plentiful.

There are so many different makes and types of PC on the market that we're going to have to keep this fairly general, and we'll confine ourselves to Pentium and Pentium-class PCs using Windows 95. In-creasing memory capacity on older PCs with 386 and 486 processors (using Windows 3.1) beyond 16 Mb, say, gives only marginal perfor-mance gains. If you have one of these machines and want to be able to use the latest software you would be better off putting your money towards buying a more up-to-date PC. We should also point out that more memory won't magically enable a 75 MHz or 133 MHz Pentium PC to run software designed for a 200 MHz MMX processor.

MEMORY UPGRADE

Begin by familiarising yourself with your PC's current memory status. It is essential that you have this information: you cannot proceed without it. You need to know how much RAM your PC has now and what sort it is. If you can't remember how many megabytes you have, open Control Panel, click on the System icon then select the General tab and it will tell you. There are lots of different types of RAM, but most recent PCs use either EDO RAM or SDRAM (see Glossary). As a general rule of thumb the chips on SDRAM modules are thinner and have more pins. It is important to get the same type when upgrading. If you're not sure check the labelling on the system box, you may find it mentioned on the instructions or even on the sales invoice, otherwise you'll have to contact the manufacturer or dealer.

You need to find out how many free memory slots there are on the motherboard. To do this you have to remove the system box lid or cover and have a look inside. Have a desk lamp or torch handy, so you can see what you are doing.

Before opening a PC we always suggest disconnecting it from the mains. Some experts advocate leaving the mains plug connected but with the socket switched off. The idea is the metal case of the PC will still be connected to earth, so any static charge you may have built up on your body and clothing will be safely dissipated, as soon as you touch the case. The contrary view is that static charges are still dissipated by the system metalwork, whether or not the case is actually earthed. Damage will only occur if a charge is discharged through vulnerable components. In either case the risks can be minimised with a few simple precautions, which we'll come to in a moment. For now we're only looking, so you can unplug the mains socket if you feel safer.

There should be a diagram or photograph of the motherboard in the motherboard manual that accompanied your PC. This will show you where the memory sockets are located. If they are obscured by ribbon cables, gently move them out of the way. Make a note of how many memory boards are installed, which sockets are occupied and the orientation of the memory boards. If your PC has 8 Mb of RAM and two memory boards, that's 4 Mb per board, and so on. Notice how the boards are kept in place: most memory sockets have little spring clips at each end. If it looks as though you are going to have to disturb some cables to get at the sockets make a sketch of where they go, or take some photographs of the innards. Replace the case or lid and check everything is working.

Your motherboard manual has other vital data, including the electrical characteristics of the memory modules. The two items we're interested in are the number of pins, and the operating voltage. The latter will be either 5 volts or 3.3 volts, if it's a newish PC. There are three pin configurations: older PCs (386 and 486s) mostly use 30-pin modules or SIMMs; some 486 and Pentium PCs use 72-pin SIMMs; most recent Pentium I and all Pentium II PCs use 168-pin memory modules, called DIMMs.

The motherboard manual should also mention memory capacity and the combinations of modules you can use. It varies from make to make but newer machines are usually more flexible. On some older motherboards it may be necessary to upgrade RAM modules in pairs. Be prepared to compromise: you may have to discard some original modules in order to get the capacity you require. You may be able to offset the cost of the upgrade by part-exchanging your old RAM modules.

You should now be able to work out the number, type and size of memory modules for the upgrade. Have this information to hand, plus the motherboard manual, when you order your memory modules. You may well be asked some additional questions. If you can't supply all the answers or there are any doubts, don't guess or take chances – pay to have the upgrade carried out by a qualified engineer.

If everything has gone according to plan you should have in front of you a small plastic bag or box containing the new SIMM or DIMM modules. Don't take them out of their packaging until they're actually needed; the plastic has been specially treated to protect the modules from static electricity. Memory chips can be destroyed by static discharged; in practice the risk is quite small but it's not worth taking any chances.

The risk increases if you work in a dry, air-conditioned atmosphere and you frequently receive small shocks or notice tiny sparks whenever you touch metal objects. In that case it's a good idea to leave your PC plugged into the mains when carrying out the upgrade, but you must switch off the supply at the socket so there are no live connections inside the box. The metal casing will still be connected to earth, however, and will safely dissipate any charge that has built up on your body or clothing.

If you're ultra cautious it's worth using an earth wrist strap. It's basically a wire with a resistive load that connects your body to earth, via the case. The company where you purchased your memory modules from should be able to supply you with one, or they can be bought from Maplin Electronics (telephone 01702 55400) for a few pounds.

Before you start make sure the PC is working properly, shut it down and remove the case or lid from the system box. Ensure there's plenty of light, so you can see what you are doing. Frequently touch or hold the case metalwork when you're working inside the case to get rid of any static build-up. Sometimes wires and cables can obscure the memory sockets; ease them out of the way and use an elastic band to stop them springing back. If you have to unplug any of them make a note of where they go, and any alignment indicators. That's especially important on the ribbon cables that connect the motherboard or expansion cards to the disk drives. One edge of the ribbon cable usually has a red marker or line. Most of the rest of the plugs have notches or lugs, so they only fit one way around.

You will probably have to remove one or more of the incumbent modules, so do that first. Socket designs vary but usually there's a small plastic or metal clip at either end. Using your fingers or the tip of a screwdriver, prise the clips outwards – only a little pressure should be needed – the module should then tip back at an angle and it can be lifted out. You may find that an adjacent module gets in the way: if so, unclip those first. Avoid touching the contacts and place the module(s) on the anti static bag or box containing your new modules. Don't get them mixed up.

Touch the case metalwork again and remove the new modules from their packaging, again try not to touch any of the contacts. Inserting the new modules is a reversal of the removal procedure; note the position of any small notches on the contact strip and the socket, so that they line up. The modules have to go in at an angle. They should seat easily – if they don't re-check the alignment and notches. Now tip the modules up to the vertical position one by one – ensure any pegs on the outside edges of the socket line up with the holes on the board – and you will hear a satisfying click as the clips engage. Check to make sure they're all seated properly, and if they are not go back and do it again. Reconnect any cables, and double-check any other plugs and sockets you may have disturbed.

You can now replace the lid. Reconnect or switch the mains back on and switch the PC on. The new memory should automatically be recognised by the motherboard BIOS. The first indication that everything has gone according to plan is a new, bigger number on the POST 'Memory Test' message that appears when the machine first boots up. Some machines may hang at this point and ask you to press a key – usually F1 – to confirm the new settings, others will continue as normal.

In the unlikely event that the PC won't boot up, or one of the disk drives doesn't work, the most likely explanation is that one of the ribbon cables has become unseated.

If you heard a series of bleeps when the machine booted up, that usually indicates that one of the memory modules is faulty, or you have fitted the wrong type. In the former case it may be possible to re-configure the BIOS. The safest thing to do, however, is contact your supplier – they may be able to talk you through it or determine the correct type of modules from the numbers or markings on your original memory boards.

Assuming everything is all right, you should find that the Windows 95/98 opening screens appear much quicker - that's another good sign. When Windows has finished loading, confirm that the machine recognises the new memory by clicking on System in My Computer, and selecting the Performance tab, where the new RAM capacity will be displayed. Give yourself a pat on the back and see what your newly turbocharged PC can do.

SOCKET OVERCROWDING

All PCs have a parallel port, and very useful it is, too. On the vast majority of computers this 25-pin socket is used by the printer; however, in recent years a growing number of other devices have appeared that also require access to a PC's parallel port. These include scanners, high capacity disk drives (Zip, Jaz etc.), video capture modules and PC-to-PC connections like DCC – (see Chapter 6). Normally connecting one extra device to the parallel port is not a problem, peripherals such as scanners and disk drives have 'through ports' that allow the printer to remain connected, but if you want to add on any more parallel port devices, the single socket on your PC simply cannot cope.

The computer industry has started to address the problem and virtually all new PCs now have USB sockets, which can support more than a hundred devices connected in a 'daisy chain'. However, it's a relatively new standard and USB peripherals such as printers and scanners are still a bit thin on the ground and usually cost a little more than their parallel port cousins. The simple short-term solution to parallel port overcrowding is to fit a second one. Most recent Windows PCs can support up to four parallel ports (designated LPT1 to LPT4). It's not difficult, it doesn't take long and it doesn't cost much, so let's do it!

INSTALLING A SECOND PARALLEL PORT

Step 1 is to make sure your PC can be fitted with an additional port (or ports). The first thing you'll need is a spare ISA expansion slot on the computer's motherboard. Many recent PCs have only two or three ISA slots to begin with so there's a chance you may not have an empty one if your machine has an internal modem, video and sound cards already fitted - the only way to find out is to remove the lid. Make sure the computer is switched off at the socket, but you might want to leave the plug in as this will ensure the metal case remains earthed. Since we're going to be fiddling around inside the machine it is a good idea to hold or touch the metal case every time you venture inside as this will dissipate any static charges that may build up on your body or clothes. The ISA slots are the longest ones on the board and usually coloured black, with a notch or gap in the middle; if you see a vacant one, you're ready to proceed. Put the lid back on and make sure everything is still working.

Step 2 is to obtain your parallel expansion card. They come in several varieties with single, double or triple ports; single and double cards generally cost less than £20 or so and can be obtained from most PC suppliers and mail order specialists advertising in computer magazines. You can peruse the instructions that come with the card, but only for amusement; they're often written in a Pidgin English that makes the average VCR manuals look a model of clarity.

In order for the card to work it must be recognised by the PC and given an identity, so Step 3 is to check your machine's resources. Right-click on My Computer, select Properties and the Device Manager tab. Make sure the computer icon at the top of the tree is highlighted and

Windows automatically detects when a new piece of hardware has
been added

double-click. This will open the Computer Properties window, showing the interrupt requests (IRQs) used by the components in your PC.
The existing parallel port (LPT1) will normally be assigned to 07. Look
for one or as many spare IRQs as your new card needs, on most
machines several IRQs between 09 and 15 are usually free.

Now for Step 4. Have a look at your parallel card; you will see several rows of 'jumpers'. The small plug-in contacts, one row (or two or
three, depending on the type of card) will be marked IRQ, with numbers next to the pins. Move the jumper (or jumpers) to coincide with
the free IRQs on your PC. Switch off the PC, remove the lid again – not
forgetting to earth yourself by touching the case – and fit the card into
the expansion slot. Replace the lid and switch the PC back on. Follow
the boot-up sequence on the screen and watch for any error messages.

For Step 5 most Windows 95/98 PCs will automatically detect the
new card and start the New Hardware Wizard. If not go to Start >

Settings > Control Panel > Add New Hardware and follow the instructions. When asked allow Windows to search for the new hardware. Windows should find the new card and automatically assign it the necessary identity (LPT 2 etc.) and resources. You can check that everything is all right by going back to Computer Properties in Device Manager as outlined in Step 3.

If all has gone smoothly the new port(s) will be up and running, ready to use. If not, here's a few things to check. Change the Parallel Port setting in the PC's BIOS to 'Auto' (refer to the manual for instructions). If you get an error message saying there is a conflict in the I/O range you will have to change the I/O jumper setting on the card; try one at a time. If the card isn't recognised by Windows ensure that it has been properly seated in the expansion socket, don't leave the card loose, use the retaining screw to keep it in place.

DVD THE NEXT GENERATION

Trying to keep up with PC technology is a bit like wrestling with a slippery snake: it's difficult to get to grips with and there's a good chance it'll turn round and give you a nasty nip. But here's a development worth keeping an eye on, it carries few risks and promises substantial benefits. It's DVD or the Digital Versatile Disk, a new type of shiny disk – the same size as an audio CD and CD-ROM – that is on course to becoming the new standard for storing and transporting computer data.

Originally DVD stood for Digital VideoDisc. It was conceived as a replacement for Laserdisc, as a carrier for movies, with superior picture and sound performance to tape. However, during the development phase manufacturers realised that the disk's massive storage capacity – currently 4.7 Gb and potentially up to 16.8 Gb – would come in quite handy for computer software. DVD-Video was launched as a home entertainment format last year and it has been very successful with several hundred disks now available and players selling for less than £200.

DVD as a PC peripheral has been slower to take off. Computer manufacturers have been offering DVD-ROM drives as an option for some time and within the past few months they've been appearing as a standard fitment on top end systems, but it has all been a bit half-hearted. The cost of DVD-ROM drives has fallen dramatically over the past year

– prices now start at less than £70 – but the format has suffered from an acute lack of software. Consequently it has mainly been of interest to those who want to watch movies on their computer screens.

Now at last the DVD software market is on the move with several major releases announced during the past few weeks of writing – more about those in a moment. DVD is also starting to have an impact as a re-writable data storage medium and affordable DVD-RAM drives are appearing in the shops. Like CD-ROM writers they can record as well as play back, but this time with the capacity to store the contents of an entire PC hard disk drive. We'll look at what DVD can do for you, as we run through the procedure for fitting a drive in your PC.

One of the main selling points for DVD on the PC is that the drives are fully backward compatible with CD-ROM, so there's no loss of functionality. You will still be able to access and use all of your current software as normal; moreover, most drives have similar performance characteristics to CD-ROM decks. DVD-ROM drives are the same size and operate in exactly the same way as CD-ROM drives and there are no specific hardware or operating system issues, though fitting one to a pre-Pentium PC using an older version of Windows (before Windows 95 and 98) might prove quite challenging.

Although DVD ROM drives can play DVD-Video disks there are a couple of points to watch out for. The PC in question will need to be a fairly fast Pentium model and in order to decode the picture and sound information additional hardware or software is required. DVD-Video data on the disk is compressed using a system known as MPEG 2 (see Jargon Filter). Software programs that can decode the data on fast Pentium class PCs are starting to appear but at the moment the most efficient solution is to fit a separate MPEG 2 decoder card to the PC. Suitable cards are supplied with some DVD-ROM kits, and as an added bonus several of them have multi-region playback, though probably not for much longer. This facility overcomes the regional coding that prevents disks sold in the USA, (Region 1) playing on DVD decks sold in Europe (Region 2). Regional coding on DVD-Video was introduced at the behest of Hollywood movie studios to give them con-trol over release dates and provide territorial control for things like soundtracks and local censorship laws. Hollywood studios have sought to close this particular loophole and decoder boards with multi-region playback are now being discontinued. In any case, it's becoming less important as the number of Region 2 titles grows and more new movie releases are appearing on DVD shortly after they debut on tape.

Watching a movie meant to be seen on a large cinema screen (or at the very least a widescreen TV) on a titchy 15-inch PC monitor isn't very satisfying, so if you're still unconvinced by DVD, two recent software releases might change your mind. They are Encyclopaedia Britannica and Encarta Reference Suite. Multimedia encyclopaedias are exactly the right type of application that can benefit from DVD and just what is needed to get the market moving. Both titles make full use of the extra capacity – previous versions were too large for a single CD-ROM – and both publishers have been able to significantly increase the video and audio content.

DVD on the PC has taken a little longer to get going than many pundits expected, but with big names like Britannica and Microsoft behind it the bandwagon has started rolling and other software companies will follow suit. It is good news for PC users: the cost of software on DVD will be no higher than CD-ROM and there are no trade-offs as far as performance or compatibility is concerned. Drives are relatively inexpensive (they cost about the same as CD-ROM drives two or three years ago) and they are easy to fit: we'll show you how in a moment.

DVD is the next big thing in home entertainment, and data storage. DVD-ROMs are now in the shops - first off the starting blocks are multimedia encyclopaedias like Britannica and Encarta, you can be sure large office suites and multimedia games won't be far behind. As an added bonus PCs with DVD drives can play DVD-Video disks, with the picture shown on the PC monitor or even your living room TV.

A recordable DVD or DVD-RAM drive is another possibility worth considering, and with a capacity of 4.7 Gb per disk, it has the potential to back up all of the data and programs on your PC's hard drive on just one or two disks. DVD drive prices are falling fast. A quick trawl through a couple of recent computer magazines revealed 'bare' EIDE type internal DVD-ROM drives (supplied without an MPEG video decoder card) selling for as little as £70. Drives with MPEG cards start at around £100; DVD-RAM drives are still a bit thin on the ground and cost from £400 or so.

INSTALLING A DVD DRIVE

Installing a DVD player in your PC is a simple and satisfying job that will not only help to stave off obsolescence a little while longer, it could even improve the functionality of your computer. The PC in question should be a reasonably recent Pentium model (133 MHz or faster) with Windows 95 or 98; while it is possible to install a DVD drive in older slower machines it's not recommended.

The procedure for installing DVD-ROM and RAM drives are basically the same and shouldn't take you more than half an hour. Before you start, however, you will need to check a few things. First, does your PC have room inside for an extra drive? (If not you can get external drives that connect to the printer port.) Normally you will leave your existing CD-ROM drive in place so you'll end up with two drives, which can be quite handy if you routinely need to access a particular CD-ROM or DVD-ROM. If you are in any doubt, whip off the lid (switch the PC off at the mains first but leave the plug in the socket) and look for an empty drive bay. You can swap the new DVD drive for your old CD-ROM, as we indicated earlier all DVD-ROM/RAM drives are backward compatible and can read all of your CD-ROMs (and play audio CDs).

While you have the case open – and remember don't touch anything – look for the data and power connectors. There should be a spare plug on the grey 'EIDE' ribbon cable that goes from the motherboard to the rear of the resident CD-ROM player (most DVD drives come with a two-way adaptor cable, in case there isn't a spare plug). The power connector is the same as the one that goes into the back of the other disk drives. It has four wires (two black, one red and one yellow). Don't worry if you can't find a spare plug; adaptor power cables are available from most PC dealers.

Lastly, check for an empty PCI socket on the motherboard. This is for the MPEG video decoder card, assuming you want to be able to play DVD-Video disks on your PC; if you're only interested in accessing CD and DVD-ROMs you should get a bare drive (you can upgrade later on). PCI sockets are usually white or grey and about three-quarters of the length of the adjacent ISA sockets.

With the PC switched off at the mains socket (but still plugged in) and lid removed, pop out the blanking plate covering the empty drive bay. It's easier to do this from inside the case, but before you go poking around touch the metalwork first to dispel any static charges. Make sure the new drive is configured as a 'slave', there should be a set of pins and shorting contact on the back (refer to the instructions) this should be in the 'S' position. If you are replacing the resident CD-ROM drive, set the shorting contact to 'M' for master. If the ribbon and power cables are long enough it's a good idea to fit them before you insert the drive into the bay. Make sure the ribbon cable is the right way around: a red marker along one edge indicates Pin 1. If you want to play audio CDs on your new drive swap over the audio lead that's plugged into the back of the CD-ROM drive. Align the drive in the frame and screw it into place. If you are installing an MPEG card, fit that now, along with any additional connecting leads, as outlined in the instructions.

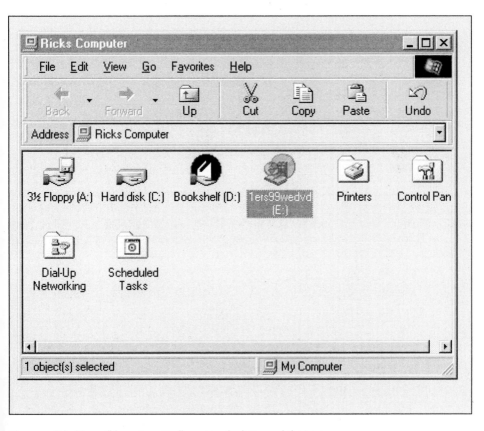

The new disk drive will be automatically assigned a letter and the icon will appear in My Computer

Switch on the PC, Windows should automatically detect the new drive and start the hardware installation wizard. If not use the Add/Remove Hardware utility in Control Panel. Follow the instructions and be ready to insert any driver and software discs as requested. Windows will assign the drive a new letter (usually E, if the C: drive isn't partitioned). It will be ready to use straight away. Your old CD-ROM drive should continue to operate as normal. It sounds easy, and it is, but if you have problems the most likely causes are badly/wrongly fitted ribbon cables, you dislodged something, or you installed the wrong driver software – so pay attention during the loading routine, and read those dialogue boxes before clicking OK!

Q&A Real world problems

Where's it gone?

Q I have a straightforward Pentium 120 PC to which I have added a Lexmark printer - that's all. It came with preloaded Windows 95, some Lotus, some vendor applications and other software. At the time I thought that a 1.07 Gb disk would more than meet my needs. I have stripped out the unwanted software, use only minimal Lotus applications and have added CompuServe 3.0.3, Netscape Communicator, PrintMaster and Encarta 97. I want to add a scanner but my system insists that I have only 85 Mb disk storage available.

Defrag tells me that I am only 1% 'defragged'. I have worked laboriously through Windows Explorer trying to size the files. The largest I can find is DiskPro at 106 Mb; everything on the hard drive comes to only 533 Mb - so where has the other 400 Mb gone?

When I contact the dealer it always seems to be my luck to get someone who talks gobbledegook at 50 mph still leaving me wondering what the answer was. Do preloaded systems come with hidden files that no one tells you about?

H. T. via e-mail

A   Explorer will miss a lot of hidden and system files and Windows 95 is notorious for commandeering free hard disk space. A large chunk has undoubtedly been assigned to the Swap File or Virtual Memory. This is a block of memory – used to store programs and data – that changes size according to the applications you are using. Normally Windows manages the virtual memory but you can elect to set the size yourself by opening the System icon in Control Panel, selecting the Performance tab and clicking on the Virtual Memory button. Even so, this is not going to win you back much space and it may slow your system down. The basic problem is the size of your hard disk drive; scanner files swallow up huge amounts of disk space and even if you recover a couple of hundred megabytes, they're not going to last very long. It's time to think about an upgrade, and while you're at it make sure you have at least 32 Mb of RAM, otherwise the scanner will operate very slowly.

Drive time

Q   I have an 18 months old Dantum 133 PC with 32 Mb RAM and have just had my 1.6 Gb hard drive upgraded to 4.3 Gb; however, the system acknowledged 2 Gb and then put the other 2 Gb as my D: drive changing my CD-ROM to the E: drive. Is there an easy way to get it all as one 4.3 Gb drive?
R. D. via e-mail

A   Windows 95 Mk I can only handle up to 2 Gb of hard disk space in a single lump; after that it splits up the extra space by creating pseudo drives or 'partitions' to which it assigns drive letters. However, a later version of Windows 95, called OSR2 (operating system, release 2) gets around this problem by recognising higher capacity drives and it makes more efficient use of the space available using a filing system called FAT32. Unfortunately Microsoft never marketed OSR2 as a stand-alone product and it is supposed to be supplied only with new PCs. Nevertheless you will find that it is readily available; have a word with your friendly local computer hardware dealer or check the small ads in computer magazines. The alternative is to upgrade to Windows 98, which uses a similar disk filing system to OSR2.

Upgrade or cast out?

Q   My company has just switched to new computers and is selling the old ones for less than £20 each. They are 486 models with 16 Mb of RAM - is it feasible to carry out an upgrade? I have seen the 486 upgrade chip from Evergreen Technologies, which will supposedly make it run like a 133 MHz Pentium PC. Assuming this works, would it be possible to run Windows 95/98? What would I need to do to use the PC in America – I am presently living in Spain – would a powerful transformer be sufficient? If all else fails, would the computer as is be okay for Internet and e-mail use?
L. C. via e-mail

A   The PCs your company is selling probably cost upwards of £1000 when new, so it does seem like a very good deal indeed, especially if it comes with a colour monitor. However, the upgrade chip you're referring to sells for around £100, and although it will improve speed and performance, Windows 95 and Windows 98 won't run anything like as fast as they would on a proper Pentium machine and some applications may not work at all. Save your money and put it towards a more up-to-date model – if that's what you need – but a 16 Mb 486 is still a useful specification, fine for word processing and similar applications and perfectly adequate for Internet use. As far as using it in the USA is concerned, a step-up transformer (110VAC to 220VAC) will work, though it's probably cheaper to fit a new power supply module; any competent PC dealer should be able to help you track one down.

Clean windows

Q   We have a family multimedia PC, which is used for both work and pleasure by everyone. We need to increase the size of the hard drive but we already have the maximum 2.1 Gb that our early version of Windows 95 allows. Should we install a newer version of Windows 95 or go the whole hog to Windows 98? Would Windows 98 create problems with newly purchased hardware such as our Agfa scanner or software including the children's games?

Most of the advice seems to suggest there are still some problems with Windows 98, but we are reluctant to purchase Windows 95 if in a few months time we need to move on again. Upgrading Windows 95 would be a cheaper option but again it seems we could experience problems.
C. B. *via e-mail*

A   A newer version of Windows won't solve your fundamental problem, which is the need for a larger hard disk drive. The logical solution would be to get a larger disk drive and Windows 98, or the OSR2 version of Windows 95, which can cope with disk drives larger than 2 Gb, without having to 'partition' or split the drive up. Most of the problems with Windows 98 have been confined to users upgrading cluttered and unstable Windows 95 PCs. Since you will be starting with a clean slate – i.e. a new hard disk drive and operating system – you should have no difficulty using your existing peripherals and software, though be warned, a few older DOS-based games have shown a dislike for the new operating system.

Drive to distraction

Q   I have an Escom P120 – well somebody has to have one .... Some time ago a friend installed a couple of memory boards for me to improve the paltry 8 Mb that I had at my disposal. All seemed fine but when we started up the PC it informed us that drive A: was not installed. On dismantling the machine we found that the lead to the A Drive had become disconnected, so we reconnected it and screwed everything back in place. However, Windows 95 told us that it could not read the floppy which we had inserted in the drive. Also the little light remains permanently on, even when the drive is empty! We tried another drive from a discarded machine, but got the same result. We asked Windows to recognise new hardware but it informs me there isn't any. Help!
B. F. *via e-mail*

A   Check to make sure you haven't inserted the ribbon connector plug the wrong way around – it can easily happen – the connectors are not 'polarised' and can go in either way. However, the more likely explanation is that you've been using the wrong plug on the ribbon cable. The one intended for Drive A: is towards the end of the cable. It's easy to identify, immediately in front of the correct plug, about one-third of the way in from the edge of the ribbon, there should be a group of seven wires, twisted through 180 degrees.

Write to life

Q I have bought a CD-writer and installed it on top of my existing CD-ROM, the idea being that I would use both and reduce wear and tear on the (expensive) CD-writer. However, I cannot seem to get any sound from the CD-ROM drive. Can you help? Does using the CD-writer for bog standard CD-ROM functions reduce its life?
R. L. via e-mail

A If you have suddenly lost the ability to play audio CDs on your original CD-ROM drive it is likely that the audio cable was dislodged during installation. It plugs into a small socket on the back of the drive, the other end goes to the sound card or a socket on the motherboard. You will only be able to hear audio CDs on one of the two drives (the one with the audio lead). In general, wear and tear is not an issue with CD-ROM drives and CD writers, there are only a few moving parts and the disk never comes into contact with the optical read/write head. You needn't worry about shortening its life by using it, in any case the technology is likely to be outmoded by DVD-ROM/RAM and other components in your PC will probably fail long before your drive will have a chance to expire.

May I interrupt?

Q Is it possible to install a second parallel port card by allowing the new card to share an IRQ, for example, with the sound card (IRQ 5) or with the existing on board parallel port (IRQ7)? With these second cards I believe that they can only use IRQ 5 or 7. Can you explain how this is done?
K. W. via e-mail

A   It is very unusual for a PC not to have at least one spare IRQ available, but in any case most secondary parallel port cards can be set to use IRQs from 3 to 15. Sharing an IRQ with another installed device is bound to cause conflicts, especially something like a sound card. Check through the IRQ allocations on your PC (right click My Computer icon and select Device Manager, then click the Properties button) to make sure that there are no uninstalled devices still allocated IRQs.

CHAPTER 11

Top tips

SCROLL CONTROL

There's a hidden feature in Word 97 that automatically scrolls the page or document you're watching. It's really handy for reading long documents, or you can use it to turn your PC screen into a teleprompter or autocue, for displaying speeches and scripts. It was originally designed to be used with 'wheel' type mice but it works on any standard two or three button mouse. Click on Customise on the Tools menu, select the Commands tab, scroll down the list and highlight 'All Commands' in the Categories window. In the right hand Commands window find, single click and hold on Auto Scroll, drag and drop it onto a toolbar and a button will appear. Close Customise and click on the Auto Scroll button, you can vary the speed and direction using the arrows that appear in the left hand scroll bar.

WINKEY SHORTCUTS

If you have a Windows keyboard you obviously know the 'Windows' button (in between Ctrl and Alt keys) brings up the Start menu, but it can do a lot more besides. Win key (Wk) + D is a very quick way of getting to the desktop as it toggles, maximise and minimise all windows. Wk + E opens Explorer, Wk + F opens Find, and Wk + R opens Run. System Properties opens with Wk + Pause, Wk + Tab steps through the programs on the Taskbar and Wk + F1 opens Windows Help.

QUICK SCREEN

If you want to launch a screen-saver quickly – maybe you're going out to lunch and want to prevent others from seeing what's on your screen – open Windows Explorer, go to the Windows folder and open the System file. There you will find all of the Windows 95/98 screen-saver files. They're easy to spot as they have monitor-shaped icons and end with the file extension *.scr. Right click on the icon, select 'Send To' then 'Desktop as Shortcut'; when you want to start it in a hurry just double-click on the desktop icon.

PRINTER HELPER

Having problems with your printer? You may be surprised to know Windows 95/98 comes with a sophisticated printer troubleshooting program. It's on the CD-ROM. You can find it with Windows Explorer: click on the D: drive icon, then open the Other folder and inside you'll find a folder called Misc, open that and then the Epts (enhanced printer troubleshooter). Click on epts.exe and the program starts, first analysing your printer set-up, it then asks a series of questions and suggests remedies to help you solve the problem.

RESTORATION JOB

Sometimes, after installing a new piece of hardware or changing your PC's video resolution settings, the desktop icons can become corrupted, or even disappear altogether. You can restore them to pristine condition by quitting Windows then re-starting in Safe mode. Press the F8 key as soon as the first boot up message appears. From the menu that appears select option 3 'Safe' mode and wait for Windows to finish loading. Exit and re-start Windows and the original desktop icons will reappear. If you use small icons on the Start menu this will need to be reset from 'Settings and Taskbar' on the Start menu.

MORE SHORTCUTS

Keyboard shortcuts are always very popular, so here's a selection for Windows Explorer: pressing F4 displays the full contents of the Address /location panel; F5 refreshes the windows, updating any changes you may have made; F6 switches the focus between the various window 'panes'.

Ctrl + A selects everything in the right-hand window, Ctrl + Z will undo the last action, and the Backspace key steps back through the parent directory tree. The asterisk key on the numeric keypad expands all of the directory branches while the '-' and '+' numeric keys collapse and expand the tree.

FASTER NET

One of the main complaints about the Internet is how long it sometimes takes to access and download pages. There's an easy way to speed things up and that is to just load text. Instead of all the pictures, graphics, advertising banners and sounds you will just see icons. If you want to see or hear an item just right click on the icon and you will get the option to load it. In Internet Explorer 3 go to View on the menu bar then Options > Advanced and uncheck the Show Pictures box. On version 4 the procedure is View > Internet Options > Advanced, scroll down to Multimedia and uncheck the appropriate boxes. A similar facility in Netscape Navigator 3 is listed under Options, simply remove the tick next to Auto Load Images; on version 4 it's listed under Preferences on the Edit menu, click Advanced and uncheck the Automatically Load Images box.

FASTER DESKTOP

Here is a nifty little trick to access the contents of your desktop from the Start button, without having to close or minimise any windows. Right click on the Start button and choose Open then on the Start Menu window that appears go to the File menu, select New and Shortcut. The Create Shortcut window opens and in the Command Line box type in the following: 'Explorer /root,' ignore the inverted commas but make sure there's a space between Explorer and the forward-slash, and don't forget the comma after root. Click Next and a window opens asking you to 'Select a title for the program'. Back space to delete the default entry and call it 'Desktop' (or anything else you fancy) and click Finish. The item should now appear on the Start menu, if you click it a window containing the contents of your desktop will open. To remove it from the Start menu go Start > Settings > Taskbar & Start Menu > Start Menu Programs tab and click the Remove button. Find the shortcut on the directory and click Remove.

QUICK DOS

If you play a lot of games on your PC or you routinely use DOS software it can be quite inconvenient to have to wait for Windows to load before you can get into the DOS mode. There's a simple way of bypassing Windows so that the PC boots straight to the DOS C: prompt. Open Windows Explorer and click on the C: drive, in the right-hand window scroll down until you find a file called Msdos.sys, right click on it and select Properties, make sure the 'Read Only' attribute is unchecked and click OK. Double-click the Msdos.sys icon and if prompted open with Notepad. Look for the line BootGUI=1, change it to read BootGUI=0 and save the file. The next time you switch on the PC it will boot to the C: prompt, to start Windows simply type 'win'.

TASKBAR TIP

Normally the contents of the Taskbar sitting at the bottom of your screen (or wherever you decided to put it) are decided for you by Windows and the applications you are running. You can take control of it and turn any folder on your PC into a Toolbar icon on the Taskbar, so you can quickly access the programs or files it contains.

All you have to do is put the mouse pointer into an empty area on the Taskbar and right-click, from the menu that appears choose Toolbars and select New Toolbar. This will open a directory tree dialogue box, choose the folder you're interested in and click OK. The folder and its contents will now be displayed on the Taskbar; you can shuffle through the folder by clicking on the little arrows.

If you want to get rid of it go back to the Taskbar menu, click on Toolbars again and de-select the item.

If the layout of your Taskbar changes don't worry, you can move the item blocks around by dragging the dividing bars with the mouse pointer.

FASTER FAVOURITES

There are probably at least one or two Internet web sites that you visit frequently – search engines or a particular home page etc. Rather than waste time opening your browser, manually selecting the address from the favourites list and making the connection, just create a simple keyboard short cut. Pressing the keys will take you straight to your chosen web site from within any application.

On the Start menu click Favourites, right-click the site you are interested in then select Properties and the Internet Shortcut tab. In the Shortcut Key box you will see 'None', click in a cursor and type a single letter – choose one that relates to the site and you can easily remember, such as 'Y' for Yahoo, etc. – the field will now display the assigned shortcut, i.e. 'Ctrl + Alt + Y'. Click OK and try it out. Internet Explorer opens automatically and takes you straight to the web site. (If Internet Explorer is not your chosen browser you will have to open it and manually add the web site address to the Favourites list.)

FONT FINDER

If you are constantly fussing over fonts for your documents then there's a very handy feature in Windows 95 and 98 that allows you to quickly compare typefaces according to style and design. From the Start menu go to Settings, then Control Panel and double click the Fonts icon. Go to the View drop-down menu and click on 'List Fonts by Similarity'. Now all you have to do is click on the drop down 'List Fonts ...', choose a font and you will be presented with a list of comparable typefaces, ranked according to similarity.

SOUNDS PERSONAL

If you're bored with Windows sounds, create your own from snippets of audio CDs, played in the CD-ROM drive. Load the CD and open the Sound Recorder by clicking on Start then Programs, Accessories and Multimedia (or Entertainment in Windows 98). Play the CD (the Audio CD player is also in Accessories > Multimedia/Entertainment) and click on the Sound Recorder red record button. You may need to adjust the level or enable the input from the CD player from Volume Control on the View menu on CD Player. Sound Recorder can also add special effects (echo, play backwards, change speed) and edit the sound (Delete Before/After on the edit menu). When you are happy with it, give it a name and save it in the Media folder in Windows. It can then easily be accessed from the Sounds utility in Control Panel and assigned to an event of your choice. Remember, no public performances if you're recording Copyright material!

BETTER BUTTONS

Windows 98 users and those with Windows and Internet Explorer 4.0 installed will have noticed the small 'Quick Launch' Toolbar on the Taskbar, next to the Start button. This is normally populated with Internet Explorer 4 and Outlook icons, but you can also drag and drop program and file icons straight on to it for even faster access. If it starts to get crowded little arrow search buttons appear or you can widen it using the separator bars. If you want to remove them later on, right click on the icon and choose delete.

SPEEDY SEND

If you compose your e-mails using Microsoft Word, or write articles then copy and paste the document into Outlook Express, you might like to know there's an easier way. Go to the File menu on Word, select Send To then Mail Recipient. This will open the Outlook e-mail window, with your document already attached – all you have to do is select the address and click Send. You have to make a couple of adjustments to Outlook Express first, however. On the Tools menu choose Options and on the General tab ensure 'Make Outlook Express my default e-mail program' is checked, then put a tick next to 'Make Outlook Express My Default Simple MAPI Client' (MAPI stands for messaging application programming interface). Restart the PC and it's done.

SPEEDY SCROLLING

The Start menu in Windows 95 can become a bit of a mess: when it becomes too large to fit on the desktop it expands sideways. It's a bit tidier on Windows 98 and the Start menu is confined to a single scrolling pane. The trouble is that the scrolling speed is quite slow and as it grows it takes longer to get from one end to the other. Fortunately there is a hidden turbocharger feature that will speed it up, just hold down the Ctrl key when you are scrolling and watch those icons fly by.

COLOUR CHANGER

Web pages can often be difficult to read especially if text colours clash with fancy backgrounds and patterns. On Microsoft Internet Explorer there's a very handy feature that will allow you to make quite significant changes to the way web pages are displayed, and in particular the colours used for web site addresses that you have and haven't visited and the so-called 'hover' colour. The latter is the colour change that occurs when your mouse pointer passes over and highlights a web address. Open Explorer and on the View menu choose Internet Options, select the General tab and click the Colours button at the bottom of the window. To change a default click on the appropriate colour block and choose a new one from the palette which appears, or create your own custom colour. A similar feature is available on Netscape Navigator on the Options menu under General Preferences.

QUICKER CONNECTIONS

Here's a quick and simple tweak that can help reduce the time it takes for your Windows 95/98 PC to make a connection to your Internet Service Provider, but only try this if it's a stand alone machine, i.e. not hooked up to a network. Open Dial Up Networking by going to Start > Programs > Accessories > Communications > Dial Up Networking. Right click on the icon for your ISP connection and select Properties and the Server Types tab. In Advanced Options uncheck 'Log on to Networks' and below that, under Allowed Networks make sure that only TCP/IP is checked. Click OK and give it a try. If all's well, Internet Explorer (or your chosen browser) should log on and establish a connection a little faster than before. In the unlikely event that anything odd happens, simply go back to Dial Up Networking and restore the default settings (i.e. Log on to Networks, NetBeui and IPX/SPX all checked).

SECOND WINDOW

On Internet Explorer 4 it is possible to open a second smaller browser window by clicking on a link, so you can still see, and quickly return to the original page without reloading it. Just hold down the shift button before left clicking on the link.

Here are some more Internet Explorer 4 keyboard shortcuts: Ctrl + D adds the current web page to your Favourite list; Ctrl + H opens the History folder; Ctrl + N opens a new browser window; Ctrl + W closes the active browser window; and Ctrl + R reloads the page you are viewing.

ICON MAKER

Bored with your desktop and all those dull-little icons? Then do something about it! You can easily create your own icons in Windows 95 and 98 using ordinary picture files or graphics created using the Paint program. You could have the pictures of the family or pets representing your programs (no jokes about using a photo of the mother-in-law to represent the word processor please) or design your own from scratch.

The image can be any size – Windows will automatically adjust the size and shape – but it must be in the Bitmap (extension .bmp) format. Most paint and graphics programs have a 'Save As' facility that will convert picture files from other file types into .bmp format. Once that's done open Windows Explorer, find the picture file and click once into the name field to highlight it, then wait a second and click again to insert a cursor so it can be renamed. Change the file extension from .bmp to .ico, and hit return. Now go to the Desktop and right-click on the icon you want to change and select Properties. On the Shortcut tab you should see a 'Change Icon' button (you can't normally change the icon on Windows applications); click it and use the Browse button to find your icon picture file, press OK and it's done.

TAME EXPLORER

Windows Explorer in Windows 95 has a mind of its own and always seems to open with a different shape, position or icon and display settings. You can make it remember your preferences – for a while at least: set it up the way you want it to look then press Ctrl + Alt + Shift when you click on the close icon (the 'x' in the top right hand corner). It will eventually forget but it's easy enough to repeat the exercise.

It's a lot easier in Windows 98, set up Windows Explorer, go to the View Menu then Folder Options and select the View Tab and press the 'Like Current Folder' button.

START STOPPER

After Windows has finished loading, other programs and applications may load automatically. These can cause problems if they become corrupted or are not removed properly, in which case you might want to prevent them starting in future. There are three locations in Windows 95/98 from where these programs are loaded.

The first is the StartUp group. Right click the Start button then Open, select the Programs icon, double-click to open and double-click on the StartUp icon. You can safely delete any of the shortcut icons shown.

Number two is a system file called Win.Ini. Select Run on the Start menu and type in 'sysedit'. Click on the Win.ini window and look under the '[windows]' entry (at or close to the top of the file) for programs listed after 'load=' and 'run='. You can remove references to programs here but be warned that Win.ini is a critical file so do not tamper with it unless you know what you are doing and have made a backup.

The third location is the Windows Registry. Once again do not fiddle around unless you have made a backup first and are confident of your abilities. Click Start then Run and type in 'regedit'. Click on the plus sign next to HKEY_LOCAL_MACHINE, then work your way down the directory tree clicking on the plus signs next to: SOFTWARE, Microsoft, Windows, CurrentVersion and Run. Entries can be removed by right-clicking on the relevant icon and selecting Delete.

BIGGER BARS

Newcomers to Windows 95 and 98 often find the scroll bars at the side and bottom of word processors and spreadsheets screens quite difficult to use. The bars are narrow and the slider can be hard to control, until you get used to it. It's easy to change the size of the bars; even seasoned users may prefer to make them a little wider. To make the change go to Control Panel, click on the Display icon and select the Appearance tab. Click in the middle of the scroll bar shown in the 'Active Window', in the display. The word 'Scrollbar' should appear in the box below marked Item, along with a pair of up/down arrows and the default setting of 16. Try 20 or 25 but if you want to see something really funny whizz it up to the maximum of 100!

FILE SQUASHER

If you are using Outlook Express and you receive and send a lot of e-mail, your Inbox and Outbox folders could be swallowing up a lot of valuable hard disk space. Get into the habit of regularly 'compacting' the files; this can also make them small enough to backup to a floppy disk. Click and highlight the selected Inbox or Outbox folder icon then go to the File menu, select Folder and Compact Folder. If you want to backup your e-mail you will find it in C:/program files/Outlook Express/Default User. Inbox and Outbox files come in pairs with '.idx' (index) and '.mbx' (mailbox) extensions, and must be copied or saved together.

YOUR OWN DEVICES

Here's a quick and easy way to open Device Manager without having to go through Settings > Control Panel > System. Right click the Start button, select Open, right click anywhere inside the open window and choose New and Shortcut. A new window will open, on the Command

Line type the following: c:\windows\control.exe sysdm.cpl, system,1
Note the full stops, commas and spaces. Now click on Next, accept the
shortcut name and select Finish. An icon called Control Exe should
now appear on the Start menu that will take you straight to Device
Manager.

INSTANT MAIL

If you are using Outlook Express as your e-mail client this handy little
trick can help to speed things up. It will put a new icon on your Start
menu. When you click on it a blank e-mail message window opens
from where you can compose and send an e-mail, without waiting for
Outlook Express to open. Move your mouse pointer to the Start button,
right click on it and select Explore from the menu that appears. When
the Explorer window opens, right click in an empty spot in the right-
hand pane and select New, then Shortcut. The Create Shortcut dialogue
box should appear; under Command Line type in 'mailto:' (leaving off
the quotation marks) then click on Next. Now you can give your shortcut a name, clear the highlighted default name and type in something
like 'e-mail' or 'messend', and select close. Now go to the Start menu
and try out your new high-speed message system.

SEND AND DELIVER

Send To is one of the most useful facilities in Windows Explorer. By
right clicking on a file, the Send To option will instantly copy the file to
another folder, a floppy disk or the clipboard, but it can do many more
things besides. You can add any application or drive destination to the
Send To list and save yourself a lot of time moving files and opening
applications.

  Go to the Start menu then Programs and open Windows Explorer.
Scroll down the list to the Windows folder, open it, locate and double
click on Send To. Now go up to File on the menu bar, select New, then
Shortcut and use Browse to find the application you are interested in.
Open the folder and look for the relevant *.exe file, single click to highlight and select Open. You will be asked to give the program a name –
if you don't want to use the default – then click Next and Finish and
the item is added to the Send To list.

LAZY LAUNCHER

Most of us are creatures of habit and once the PC has booted up to the Windows desktop we normally open the same applications every time. Why bother? Windows can do it for you, automatically, launching any program you choose.

Go to the Start button, then Programs and scroll down the list until you come to Start Up, click the right mouse button and select Open. Now you can drag and drop the icon of your chosen program from the desktop into the open Start Up window. If you want to keep the icon on the desktop hold down the Ctrl key when you click on the icon, this makes a copy and leaves the original where it is. If your program isn't on the desktop, open Windows Explorer and open the application folder. Look for the program's '.exe' file, highlight then click on copy (or Ctrl + C) and paste (Ctrl + V) it into the Start Up window. To delete a program from Start Up use the Remove facility on the Taskbar and Start Menu item that can be found in the Settings folder on the Start menu.

CARD SHARP

The Solitaire game in Windows must be one of the greatest time-wasters of all time – it drives office managers crazy – but even though it is so simple it can be highly addictive. If you're one of the millions hooked on it then you have probably figured out by now that the Draw 3 option – selected by default – slows the game down, increases the odds against you winning and makes it harder to play. Of course you could just switch to easy-peasy Draw 1 setting and play it that way, but where's the fun in that? The next time you're in a fix try this simple little cheat: press and hold down the Ctrl, Alt and Shift keys, then click on the top card and you'll find that you can now select cards one at a time.

Glossary

286, 386, 486
Families of Intel microprocessor chips developed during the 1980s and early 1990s. Forerunners of the Pentium chips used in the latest PCs.

AVERY LABELS
A range of standardised label styles and formats, developed by the office equipment company of the same name.

BETA
Beta software is usually a near-final version of a program or application, made available to testers and volunteers on an at-their-own-risk basis, to help identify any last remaining bugs, glitches and conflicts.

BIOS
Basic Input Output System. A set of instructions that tells your PC what it is connected to, and how to communicate with devices such as disk drives and memory chips.

BITMAP
Picture file format used by Windows and many PC applications.

BROWSER
An Internet access program, such as Microsoft Internet Explorer or Netscape Navigator.

CELL
A spreadsheet table is divided into boxes or cells, each of which is assigned a unique identity code. A cell can contain a mixture of text, numbers and mathematical formulae.

CLIP ART
Copyright-free pictures, icons, cartoons and graphics supplied with word processor programs, or available separately on disk or from thousands of web sites on the Internet.

COBOL
Common Business Oriented Language. A programming language used in data processing and business applications.

COMPRESSION
A technique to reduce the size of a file, to make it smaller, more manageable, easier to store and move around.

CORDLESS LINK
PC communication systems that do not involve the use of wires, i.e. data is sent by infra-red light or radio signals.

CPU
Central Processor Unit. The main microprocessor chip in a PC.

CROPPING
Trimming the edge of an image, so that it fits the space allocated.

DATA CARTRIDGE
A tape cassette, similar to an audio or video tape. (Some tape backup systems use DAT and 8 mm audio and video cassettes.)

DATE FIELD
A simple line of computer code, embedded in a document, that automatically inserts today's date into a letter.

DECOMPRESS
Files sent over the Internet are often 'compressed' to make them smaller and faster to send. However, in order to use the files they have to be decompressed or extracted on the host PC. Some compressed files come with their own automatic extraction utility, others – usually with the extension *.zip – depend on a separate program on the PC to 'unzip' the files.

DEFRAGGING
Over time the files on a PC's hard disk drive become disorganised. 'Defragging' the drive restores order and speeds up reading and writing data.

DESK-TOP PUBLISHING (DTP)
Desk-top publishing programs are designed with page layout in mind. The emphasis is on moving and manipulating text, graphics and photographs, though pretty well all of them have word processing facilities as well.

DIRECTORY TREE

A graphic representation of the way folders and files are stored on your PC's disk drives. In Windows Explorer, clicking on the '+' sign to folders opens up 'branches' of sub-directories containing files and folders.

DCC

Direct Cable Connection. A Windows 95/98 utility for connecting two PCs together so they can exchange files.

DIMM

Dual In-line Memory Module. Usually with 168 connecting pins.

DLL

Dynamic Link Library. Data files used by one or more programs.

DOCUMENT TEMPLATE

A document template is a largely blank page containing basic text, layout and style formatting instructions that you may want to re-use over and again.

DOMAIN

The unique name or address given to a server computer connected to the Internet, i.e. www.telegraph.co.

DMA

Direct Memory Access. A means of transferring data quickly between the hard disk and the PC's memory.

DRIVERS

Small programs that tell Windows how to communicate with internal hardware, such as disk drives, and peripherals such as printers, scanners etc.

DVD

Digital Versatile Disk. New high-capacity optical disk system with a capacity of up to 5.2 Gb per disk (at the moment). DVD drives can also read CD-ROMs. DVD recordable or 'RAM' drives have recently come onto the market.

DVD-RAM

Digital Versatile Disk – Random Access Memory. Re-writable DVD system where data on disks can be recorded and erased many times.

EDO RAM

Extended Data Out, Random Access Memory. High-speed RAM chips used on recent PCs with specialised memory controllers.

E-MAIL ATTACHMENT
An attachment is a file – other than plain text – sent with or as an e-mail message.

EIDE
Enhanced Integrated Drive Electronics. Data interface and control system used by most current disk drives.

ENCRYPTION
Encryption or scrambling renders files unreadable by any conventional means without the correct decryption software and a unique 'key' code, which is needed to unlock the data.

ENGINE
A self-contained program designed to do a specific task that operates within a larger application.

FAQ
Frequently Asked Questions. A simple guide to a particular topic or subject area.

FILE FRAGMENTS
Files or bits of files left behind on the hard disk when a program is deleted.

FLAME
Literally to be 'shot down in flames'. Offensive or abusive e-mails, usually sent in response to someone infringing basic newsgroup netiquette.

FLIP and ROTATE
The facility in paint-box programs and some word processors to turn an image or object on the page.

FOLLOW-UPS
A response to a newsgroup message or posting which will form part of a 'thread' for others to read and reply to.

FONT/TYPEFACE
Text style and size. Virtually all word processors have a 'wizzywig' display (actually WYSIWYG, or what you see is what you get), so what appears on the screen is what ends up on the printed page.

FORMULA
Mathematical expressions, such as add, subtract, multiply and divide, used

to create an instruction that tells a cell how to behave or process a piece of information.

FREEWARE
Shareware programs that are free to use, but the author retains control and copyright over the original programming code.

GAMMA CORRECTION
A means of jiggling brightness values in an image to compensate for the non-linear characteristics of PC and video monitors. In other words a way of making sure that a picture or photograph on a video screen looks the same as the paper original.

GPF
General Protection Fault. Conflict over 'protected' memory allocated by Windows to running programs.

GSM
Grams per square metre. A measurement of the weight and to some extent the thickness of paper and card. Your printer's instruction book will contain details of its paper handling capabilities.

HOT KEYS
A combination of two or three keys strokes that activates a command or a program.

HTML
HyperText Mark-up Language. Hidden or embedded codes, commands and formatting instructions in a text document or Internet web page that help a browser to move around inside the document, or direct it to other web sites or addresses.

HTTP
HyperText Transfer Protocol. A set of rules used that governs how text is displayed on Internet documents plus a means of moving around inside documents and accessing other web pages by clicking on highlighted or underlined links.

INBOX
A folder created by Outlook Express where all of your incoming mail messages are stored.

IRQ

Interrupt Request. A signal from a device connected to a PC motherboard – such as an expansion card – asking the central processor to send receive or process data.

ISA

Industry Standard Architecture. Type of expansion card socket common to all IBM PC computers, used for sound and video adaptors, PC TV tuners, etc.

ISP

Internet Service Provider. Company providing individuals with Internet access. Until recently most ISPs charged a monthly subscription though a growing number of ISPs now provide free access.

JPEG

Joint Photographic Experts Group. Compressed picture file format used for photographic images.

KEY CAPS

Press-fit embossed keys tops on a PC keyboard.

LAN

Local Area Network. A computer network where all of the PCs are physically close to one another, in the same room, office or building.

LASERDISK

Now virtually obsolete, the limited storage capacity of the LP-sized disks meant films had to be recorded on both sides of the disk or on two disks.

LCD

Liquid Crystal Display. Flat panel display used on laptop and portable PC and now available for desktop machines. LCD monitors consume far less power than the cathode ray tube type and generate no harmful emissions.

LUMINANCE

The brightness component in a picture, photograph or image on a PC monitor.

MAILBOX

Storage space on an ISP's server computer where incoming e-mail messages are stored prior to them being downloaded and read on your PC.

MIME

Multipurpose Internet Mail Extensions. A widely used system for converting non-text files and information – images, HTML commands etc. – to and from plain text so it can be sent as e-mail.

MODEM

MOdulator/DEModulator. A device that converts digital signals coming from your PC into audible tones that can be sent via a conventional telephone line.

MOTHERBOARD

The main circuit board inside a PC containing the CPU and its support circuitry, with sockets for memory cards and the sound, video and input/output 'daughter boards'.

MPEG 2

Motion Pictures Expert Group. A division of the International Standards Organisation.

MS-DOS

Microsoft Disk Operating System. Core control program that functions alongside Windows, uses text-based 'command lines' to carry out instructions.

NAG SCREEN

A window or display that appears when a program has started to remind the user to pay a registration fee or indicate how many days of the trial period remain.

NEWSGROUP

Public noticeboards on the Internet where like-minded net users can post e-mail messages, articles or announcements for others to read and respond to.

NIC

Network Interface Card. A plug in card that fits into one of the PC's mother-board expansion sockets. NICs are also available in the form of PC cards, for use in laptops.

NOS

Network Operating Software. A program running on a network server computer. The best-known NOS programs are Novell Netware, OS/2 Warp Server, Open Server and Windows NT Server.

NUMBER FORMAT
A set of styles, that decides how numbers, symbols and mathematical expressions are presented.

ON-SCREEN KEYBOARD
A virtual keyboard where characters are selected using a mouse pointer or other means, such as voice control or movement.

OPERATING SYSTEM (OS)
A collection of programs, such as Windows 95, 98 and DOS (disk operating system) that manages all of your PC's resources – RAM memory, disk-drive, display screen, etc. – and controls how files are stored and retrieved.

PAPER WEIGHT
The weight and thickness of paper is expressed in grams per square metre (gsm). Ordinary photocopier/printing paper is usually around 85 gsm, greetings card paper in the range 200 to 300 gsm.

PAPER PATH
The rollers and guides inside a printer through which sheets of paper pass.

PARALLEL PORT
One of the rear panel connections on your PC (or laptop) usually used by printers and scanners. Data is transferred relatively quickly 4 or 8 bits at a time.

PATCH
A program or file intended to fix or work around a problem in a software application.

PCI
Peripheral Component Interconnect. High-speed connector and control system, used on most recent PCs. Also used for sound, video, and adaptor cards.

PCX
Picture Exchange format. A type of common image file, used by a number of drawing packages, allowing files to be easily exchanged.

PIXEL
Picture Element. The basic building block in computer imaging, effectively a single dot on the screen or printout. The greater the number of pixels in an image the finer the resolution.

POP3

Post Office Protocol version 3. Widely used Internet e-mail standard, compatible with popular Windows 'client' software (Outlook, Outlook Express, MS Exchange/Windows Messaging, Eudora etc.) on PCs and palmtop computers.

POST

Power On Self-Test. A small diagnostic program that operates every time you switch your PC on, to make sure everything is working correctly.

REGISTRY

A large, constantly changing file in Windows 95 and 98 containing details of how your PC is set up and configuration information for all the programs stored on the hard disk.

RESIZING

Changing the physical size of an image or object on the page, usually by dragging a sizing square, so that it fits into a space.

SATURATION

Colour intensity, changing the saturation on a photograph is like altering the colour control on a television, and like a TV it can be varied from zero (black and white) to far too much.

SDRAM

Synchronous Dynamic Random Access Memory. Another family of memory chips that allows data to be accessed at higher speeds.

SEARCH ENGINE

Internet sites that seek out information, by topic, keyword or name. Good places to start are www.yahoo.com, www.lycos.com, www.altavista.com.

SERIAL PORT

Most PCs have two serial ports. One may be used by the mouse, the other by an external modem. Data is transferred relatively slowly, one bit at a time.

SERVER

Fast, powerful computers with vast storage capacity, used to communicate and share data with other computers connected to local or large-scale networks.

SHAREWARE

Software programs that you can try before you buy. If you decide to use it you are obliged to send a payment to the author or publisher. Some programs are automatically disabled when the trial period has expired.

SIMM

Single In-Line Memory Module. With 30 or 72 connecting pins.

SOUND CARD

A more or less standard fitment on modern desktop PCs, generating the sounds and music heard through the PC's speakers. Most sound cards also have a microphone input, necessary for voice recognition.

SYSTEM FILES

Important files (Autoexec.bat, config.sys, command.com, win.ini etc.) containing text-based commands, that set up and configure Windows and the programs running on the PC.

TEMP FILES

Temporary files, ending in '.tmp' are created by Windows and other programs and normally deleted automatically, though some will remain if Windows crashes or is not shut down properly.

TEMPLATE

A template is a page that contains embedded instructions concerning typeface and size, page layout and style features. Word processors such as Microsoft Word contain a wide selection of ready-made templates, or you can create your own.

THUMBNAIL PREVIEW

Reduced sized image, quicker to load and display and cuts down on memory resources.

TIME-LIMITED

Programs with a built-in time switch, that will stop it functioning after a pre-set period – usually 30 days – after it was installed.

TOOLS

Small programs or applications that modify or change the way things work or happen on a PC.

TRACKBALL

A kind of upside-down mouse, where screen pointer movement is controlled by moving a large ball.

UNINSTALLER

A program removal utility included with a lot of Windows software;

programs with uninstallers are usually (but not always) listed in Add/Remove Programs in Control Panel.

URL
Uniform Resource Locator. A standardised address format for Internet web sites.

USB
Universal Serial Bus. Industry standard connection system for peripherals (modems, joysticks, printers etc.) that does away with confusing technicalities and allows 'hot swaps', allowing connection and disconnection with the PC switched on.

USENET
A network of server computers used to distribute the 'official' newsgroups on the Internet.

VGA
Video Graphics Array. Standard display format used on PCs, typically made up of 640 × 400 pixels and 256 colours.

VOICE SYNTHESISER
Software that converts text – including menu options and commands – appearing on the PC screen into speech.

WET CLEANERS
Disk drive cleaners that use a liquid agent (usually isopropyl alcohol) to remove dirt and dust from the read/write heads or laser pickups.

WIZARD
A self-activating program that guides you through a simple set-up routine for a particular feature or application.

WORDBASIC
Simple text-based programming language used by Word, to control various behind-the-scenes functions and features (BASIC = beginners all-purpose symbolic Instruction Code).

Index